TAKE THE
HIGH ROAD

TEN YEARS OF

TAKE THE
HIGH ROAD

MICHAEL
ELDER

SCOTTISH TELEVISION

Boxtree

First published in the UK 1990
by BOXTREE LIMITED, 36 Tavistock Street,
London WC2E 7PB

1 3 5 7 9 10 8 6 4 2

Edited by Anne Scott
Designed by Sarah Hall
Cover designed by Threefold

Typeset by Cambrian Typesetters, Frimley, Surrey
Origination by Culver Graphics
Printed in Italy by Imago Publishing Limited

British Library Cataloguing in Publication Data

Elder, Michael
    10 years of "Take the High Road".
    1. Television programmes: Soap operas
    I. Title
    791.45

    ISBN 1–85283–109–X

For ten years many people have made Take the High Road *possible.*
Some of their names and faces appear herein.
Many do not. Without them all there would be no programme
and so no book which is therefore warmly dedicated to them.

CONTENTS

'TAK THE HIGH ROAD'   9

INTRODUCTION   10

1 THE STORY BEHIND *TAKE THE
   HIGH ROAD*   12

2 THE MAKING OF *TAKE THE HIGH
   ROAD*   23

3 IT HAPPENED IN GLENDARROCH   32

4 THE CHARACTERS AND WHO
   PLAY THEM   48

   THE FUTURE   95

   IN MEMORIAM   96

'TAK THE HIGH ROAD'

By yon bonnie banks and yon bonnie braes,
Where the sun shines bright on Loch Lomon',
Where we hae passed sae mony happy days
On the bonnie, bonnie banks o' Loch Lomon'.

O ye'll tak the high road and I'll tak
    the low road
And I'll be in Scotland afore ye.
But trouble it is there and mony hearts are sair
On the bonnie, bonnie banks o' Loch Lomon'.

The strange words of this most popular of
Scots songs have a very real meaning. They
are reputed to have been written after the
Jacobite Rising of 1745 by prisoners awaiting
execution in Carlisle Jail. Most of these prisoners were Highlanders and there is an old
Highland belief that the soul of a Highlander
who died outwith his native country travelled
home underground. Hence those who were to
be released would travel home above ground –
the high road – while those condemned to
death would travel home underground – the
low road. The latter would consequently get
home first.

INTRODUCTION 1

By Robert Love, Executive Producer

When Gwyneth Guthrie (Mrs Mack) appeared not long ago as a guest on BBC's *Open Air* programme, she replied to one of her phone-in questioners by saying, 'It's nice to have our own *Scottish* soap . . . ,' and went on to point out to the caller from the South of England that *Take the High Road* is shown at tea-time in Scotland and therefore goes out along with 'the fish and chips . . .' In other words, a Scottish institution? Certainly the Scottish audience behaves very proprietorially towards it, as witness the furore that greeted the recent changes we decided to make to take the series into the Nineties. We hope we got it right.

Take the High Road is unique among British soap operas for several reasons. It has, for example, more exterior sequences per episode than any of its rivals. Well, of course it has a much more scenic background than any of the others. It is also about a wider range of characters than the other soaps, encompassing as it does the whole gamut of social classes (not just the people in a suburban street or square). Women have always had a prominent, not to say dominant, role in *Take the High Road*, not something that can necessarily be said of some of the other serials. And it is the only soap opera on the ITV network which is produced by a regional ITV company.

How will it meet the challenges of the new television age of the Nineties? It will certainly look brighter and probably be more youthful in tone. The storylines will move faster, and perhaps be a little spicier! Essentially, however, it will retain the qualities which have endeared it to a loyal audience throughout the United Kingdom – warmth, charm and its own quirky brand of humour.

INTRODUCTION 2

By Brian Mahoney, Producer

By one of those wild coincidences that you can only get away with in real life, my wife and I brought up our family on an island in Loch Lomond – leading 'the good life', one might say, before it was fashionable. Ironically, the success of *Take the High Road* put a stop to all that and we had to go back to the city. That experience and thirty years of making television stand me in good stead anywhere from Auchtarne to Glendarroch.

A continuous serial is more than a full-time job for the producer. It is a way of life. Planning, editing, budgeting, writing, acting and performing, all have problems which come daily through your office door, together with less tractable matters like having to ask Miss X to lose a few pounds or informing Mr Y delicately that he should see an optician. It helps if you have an opinion on the probable effect of the withdrawal of hill sheep farming subsidies by the EEC; how Willie should say the third speech on page 27 so that it doesn't get a laugh; will it rain on the 22nd August and what is the price of cheese north of Inveraray?

We have a good team, of course. The job would be impossible unless everyone contributed one hundred and ten per cent. The illusion of Reality must be maintained against the background of a quite different Reality and, over the years, many come and many go for many different reasons. I remember once asking an old minister if he got bored during the thirty-odd years he had been in his remote Highland charge. 'Never,' he replied. 'It has been like preaching to a procession.' *Take the High Road* seems to me to be a long and ever-changing procession to which I am, at one and the same time, Routemaster and Honorary Uncle. No wonder my hair has gone grey, but it is a small price to pay for 'the good life' in Glendarroch.

ONE

THE STORY BEHIND
TAKE THE HIGH ROAD

Take the High Road is unique amongst British soap operas in that from the day it started to the present it is the only one produced by a regional television company for regular national transmission. It is also not generally realised outside Scotland that Scottish Television has a long record of soap opera production for transmission within its own area. Over many years before the arrival of *Take the High Road* Scottish Television produced no less than three different soaps. Firstly, in 1968 there was *High Living*, the story of a group of families and individuals living in one of Glasgow's high-rise blocks. This was immensely popular and ran for nearly 200 episodes, ending its once weekly run in late 1971. After *High Living* closed a spin-off series was mounted, based on the life of one of the series's most popular characters who began to run her own business. The series was called *A Place of Her Own* and was slightly more upmarket than its predecessor: the launderette was replaced by a smartly equipped office, the council flats by grander apartments. *A Place of Her Own* did not have a very long life and was followed by a series set in a central Scottish mining town and called *Garnock Way* which was transmitted once a week for a total of over 300 episodes.

Garnock Way was at the height of its popularity in Scotland when the Independent Television Authority, as it then was, made it known that it was prepared to consider suggestions for a daytime soap opera to be shown on the network and which they hoped would be mounted by a company other than one of the Big Five. With its experience in producing series for Scotland, Scottish Television was in a strong position to take up the challenge for this space, and work began on trying to find a suitable subject which would provide enough potential stories to last for many hundreds of episodes. At one point it was hoped that perhaps *Garnock Way* might fill the bill, but it was felt that the Scottishness of the programme was too strong for consumption outside Scotland.

Brian Izzard was Head of Entertainment at Scottish Television at the time and he was put in charge of accepting this challenge. Izzard asked Don Houghton to research the background, to suggest stories and to prepare a dossier from which a pilot programme could be made to show to the network.

Don Houghton has a long track record as a writer of all kinds of television series. No one could have been better qualified to originate something of this kind. His research was to be absolutely invaluable to the new series, as was his advice on how to set the thing up and keep it going. He wrote for it for several years before other things began to take up more of his time, and many of the characters he originated still appear in the programme.

What form would the new soap opera take? Discussions were long and serious. This was important. Never before had a regional company been invited to provide a soap opera for the network, to compete with the major programming companies for space in the schedules. It was a radical change of policy, not altogether popular with the Big Five companies, and it was vitally important that Scottish Television got it right. For one thing, it must be better than any rivals in order to clinch the spot available in the schedules. Although three of the successful applicants would have their product shown for a limited period, there was little chance that more than one of them would be given the opportunity to continue into the future. Secondly it must be seen to be a fine product in its own right which could not be written off as not up to standard.

All soap operas have a central core. The core may vary. It can be a place of work – *General Hospital, Emergency Ward 10, Crossroads*. It can be an urban area – *Coronation Street, Eastenders, Brookside*. Or a geographical location – *Emmerdale*. It was this last which provided the ideal background for a Scottish soap, and what a background. The scenery. The scenery had to be exploited: the pictures of mountain and loch and heather which sell millions of calendars each year and are dear to the hearts, not only of Scotsmen and women all over the world, but of many other people as well. That was the romantic background against which a practical story of everyday problems would be set. And so the idea of an estate in the Highlands almost automatically sprang to mind as the central

core. There was immediate drama in the situation. Most estates in Scotland at the time were facing severe financial hardship. Many were being sold to rich entrepreneurs from abroad because the traditional owners, under the pressure of swingeing taxation, could no longer afford to run them. The Highland estate was essentially feudal in it basis. On the estate were the crofts and farms and the people who drew their living from working the land. There was also the local village with its enclosed community, its local shop and its church.

Village. Farms and crofts. The Big House. There were three threads here which could be interwoven to form the basis for a successful and long-running series.

The next thing to be considered was the location. To begin with Scottish Television would have to mount a pilot programme, a single episode to show to the network controllers for approval, but it was natural that this pilot programme should be set in the same place as the final series. One aspect exercising many minds was the degree of Scottishness to use. Ten years ago, people in the south were not so ready to accept a 'foreign' dialect as they are today. There was an in-built belief in the Home Counties that if it was Scots it would be incomprehensible. Therefore wherever the programme was set it would be unwise to employ the broad accents of either Edinburgh or Glasgow or indeed of any part of the Central Belt of Scotland. But a *Highland* setting was a different matter. Highland English is amongst the purest spoken, instantly comprehensible to even the most Anglophile viewer.

That decision taken, where would the outside location work be done? This was governed by a question of geography. Union rules lay down a maximum distance within which technicians may travel before they have to be paid overnight expenses, and Scottish Tele-

Work on location is a very important, though sometimes uncomfortable, part of *Take the High Road*. Here the camera crew line up a shot on Archie Menzies (Paul Kermack), and the weather looks reasonable.

vision was anxious to avoid working outside that area. Not only would the question of getting from base to location be extended in time, but also the cost would entail serious curtailment of the amount of filming. Fortunately the ideal choice lay just within the range of permissible travel. The picturesque village of Luss nestles at the side of Scotland's most famous loch, Loch Lomond. All the ideal locations were within easy distance of the village. And so Luss became Glendarroch.

The basic decisions were made. But all was not to be plain sailing from then on.

The pilot programme was made in the summer of 1979 and on the basis of what was presented in it, the network offered Scottish Television twenty-six episodes to be transmitted twice a week and to run alongside two other successful contenders, *Together* from what was then Southern Television and *Taff's Acre* from HTV.

Perhaps it is true of all soap operas that, because of the extreme pressure of producing so many episodes over so long a period, work proceeds by a series of jumps from crisis to crisis. *Take the High Road* is certainly no exception. The first crisis happened shortly after the pilot programme had been accepted by the network controllers. A national technicians' strike closed down studios and wrecked filming schedules all over the country.

The strike began in August 1979 and lasted until October. It was universally damaging, but it struck *Take the High Road* at the worst possible time. Most of the preparatory work on the programme had to be suspended. When the strike was settled two precious months had been lost – and the network still wanted the programme for transmission the following February. Fortunately the planning of the programme had gone ahead during the strike, and in spite of the bleak outlook for actually putting anything on videotape, the form of the new series was hammered out.

Originally the title had been *The Glendhu Factor* (factor in the sense of the Scottish noun meaning estate manager.) This was abandoned for several reasons. For one thing, BBC Scotland was at that time making a drama series called *The Omega Factor*. There was also the ever-popular *The Krypton Factor*. A third 'Factor' was one too many. Another title had to be found. What about using the name of the place for the series – *Glendhu*, which in Gaelic means the black valley? But *Glendhu* sounded odd. The Scots word for a pigeon is a doo, and there were obvious and unwanted comic possibilities in the name. (Had not a recent BBC Scotland serial called *The Haggard Falcon* been nicknamed *The Battered Budgie*? And the skean dhu, the black knife worn in the stocking with Highland dress, is sometimes described as a pigeon enjoying the winter sports at Aviemore). It might also sound odd to English ears – even without the 'Doo' factor. So the name of the village had to be changed. Due to the increased output of the station, the Department of Entertainment which Brian Izzard had headed at Scottish Television had recently been split into two distinct categories – Drama and Light Entertainment. The recently appointed Head of Drama at Scottish Television and executive producer of the new series, Robert Love, suggested *Glendarroch*, because Darroch was his mother's maiden name. Glendarroch was accepted as the name of the small Highland village and the estate but not as the title of the programme. But as the outside work was to be filmed at Luss on Loch Lomond, it was an easy step to connect the programme with the song, 'The Bonnie Banks o' Loch Lomon',' and the title *High Road Low Road* became a strong contender. It was abandoned because few people could pronounce it easily. But by a process of fairly logical steps the final title *Take the High Road* was reached.

Having a title was all very well, but how was the network's deadline for the programme to be met? As the strike dragged on, Scottish Television's longed-for chance of getting a major series on the network seemed to be fast disappearing. If the series was to stand a real chance of being up and running by mid-February 1980 what was urgently needed was planning of schedules, allocation of film crews, organisation of studio space and studio crews, booking of actors, commissioning of writers, appointment of directors. None of this could happen until it was known when the strike would be over and definite dates and times could finalised.

But certain other executive decisions could be made.

Clarke Tait was appointed producer of the new series. Clarke had trained as an actor, then became a Scottish Television cameraman before moving into the field of direction. He was an abrasive character with a tremendous driving force, a sure knowledge of all the pitfalls, both technical and artistic, which the making of any drama series inevitably throws up, and an amazing store of energy. It was a wise appointment. His kind of gritty determination and no-nonsense approach were badly needed to get the floundering programme to the screen. Clarke had very definite ideas and imposed them on the series wholeheartedly. In his day no one was allowed to refer to *Take the High Road* as a 'soap opera'. The term, he said, was inaccurate and out of date. It arose from the days when early radio and television series in the United States were sponsored by commercial companies, usually soap manufacturers. It was meaningless in this country and tended to be used by those who were contemptuous of what long-running series stood for. *Take the High Road* was a series. Not a soap.

After eighty-two episodes of *Take the High Road* Clarke was appointed Head of Light Entertainment at Scottish Television and the job of producer of the programme fell to Brian Mahoney who, after working in the theatre, principally and coincidentally in the old Gateway Theatre where *Take the High Road* was made, had joined Scottish Television as a floor manager almost at the time of its formation in 1957. From there he had risen rapidly to become a much-respected director of many different types of programme, including *Take the High Road*. This was to be his greatest challenge as *Take the High Road* steadily expanded its number of episodes. It says much for his staying power that he took over at Episode 83 and is still there, still as cheerful and incisive as he was at the start.

Clarke Tait's tenure of his new post did not last very long. He died very suddenly at the age of forty-eight.

The first script editor on *Take the High Road* was Victor Carin, a very well-known Scottish actor who had run the repertory theatre at the Gateway for a couple of seasons in the early 1950s and played a leading role in *A Place of Her Own*. He had also done a great deal of writing for radio and television and two of his adaptations for the theatre, *The Servant o' Twa Maisters* from Goldoni and *The Chippit Chantie* from Molière, beautifully translated into old Scots, are still occasionally performed with great success. Victor had begun to feel dissatisfied with acting and wanted to turn more and more to writing. The job as script editor was one which seemed to him to answer all his aspirations and he looked forward to it with great enthusiasm. Alas, almost as soon as he started the job he fell ill and although he struggled to continue he was never able to fulfil it in the way he wanted to. Eventually he had to leave the programme and he died a few months later at the same age as Clarke Tait. Victor was sadly missed and his departure from the programme provided *Take the High Road* with its second crisis as the strike ended

Take the High Road's first producer Clarke Tait, barely recognisable in a dinner jacket, holding a couple of awards some time after he had left the programme to become Scottish Television's Head of Light Entertainment.

Right, Victor Carin was for many years a highly respected actor and writer before he became the first script editor of *Take the High Road*. This is a publicity shot of him as he appeared in an earlier Scottish Television soap opera, *A Place of Her Own*.

at last and technical planning for the twenty-six episodes which the network had asked for began. Script editing had perforce to be taken over by an unofficial committee.

It had been hoped that it might be possible to run *Garnock Way* in parallel with *Take the High Road*, *Garnock Way* for purely Scottish consumption, *Take the High Road* for a wider audience, but the strike and other factors made this impossible. There simply weren't the facilities to run two such series at the same time. The cast of *Garnock Way* were gathered in the rehearsal room at the Gateway and over coffee and biscuits provided by the management, were told that the programme had been axed. To this day actors still say when they are asked to a Scottish Television get-together, 'If there are coffee *and* biscuits it'll be bad news.'

The axing of *Garnock Way* was sudden and a great shock to the artists and the writers, but it was mitigated a little by the fact that several of the *Garnock Way* cast transferred to *Take the High Road*. This was particularly the case with Bill Henderson who had played the drunken miner Tod Baxter in *Garnock Way* and who in the pilot programme and for a long time in the planning of *Take the High Road* was to turn up in the village store as an alcoholic escaping from his past. The part was actually called Tod Baxter in the pilot script, but this was changed before the programme went out on the air to Ken Calder, and although the mysterious history of alcoholism remained as a throwback to the original character from *Garnock Way*, all other connections disappeared. Other *Take the High Road* favourites who were also in *Garnock Way* were Eileen McCallum who now plays Isabel Blair – Eileen played Jean Ross in *Garnock Way* – and Paul Kermack (Archie Menzies) played Jock Nesbit, some people say in the same cap! John Stahl (Inverdarroch) played PC Scoular, and several other *Garnock Way* stalwarts have also appeared in *Take the High Road*.

While *Garnock Way* was consigned to oblivion Don Houghton was issuing breakdowns for the first episodes of the new series. Breakdowns are a resumé of what each scene in each episode should contain, the characters involved and whether the scene is to be filmed outside or set in one of the four available studio sets in the Gateway. The first writers were engaged. Don wrote the first six episodes himself to set the pattern, the tone and the style. But shortage of time was becoming a worrying factor. Filming had to take place a month before the studio work was done to allow time for the processing and editing of the film scenes. In spite of heroic efforts, it wasn't possible to start filming until after Christmas and the New Year were past, which meant that the studio work could not start until the beginning of February. And the programme had to be on the air a fortnight later. It was all horribly close.

There were times when Don was writing the film scenes a day or two before they were due to be shot, without having any idea of what the studio scenes interspersed between them were going to consist of. One script writer turned up in the office with his first script shortly before Christmas and said, 'Incidentally, I've added a dog, a cat, a sheep and a cow to the story. I hope that's all right.' Clarke Tait's response was, 'You expect us to worry about animals when we haven't even got the actors yet?' His actual words were a little more colourful.

In the office Margaret Bisset and Elizabeth Condie, the two production secretaries were literally typing scripts with one hand and answering telephones with the other. Maggie was with the programme when it started, having guided *Garnock Way* through its life, and Liz joined very soon afterwards. Even after the move from the Gateway to the big studio in Glasgow, they followed the show and are still with it. Over the transition period

Margaret Bisset and Elizabeth Condie in the *Take the High Road* office. Maggie and Liz, together with Pat Daly and Aileen Roy, handle all the secretarial and administrative work of the programme.

between Edinburgh and Glasgow they were joined in the office by Pat Daly. Later Aileen Roy was appointed as chief logician whose unenviable job is trying to work out where each actor is supposed to be on which day: whether out on location filming, in the studio recording or in the rehearsal room rehearsing next week's episodes. People tend to think that the administrative staff behind the scenes in a soap opera is enormous, maybe a dozen secretaries working in spacious offices, but on *Take the High Road* in the early days Maggie and Liz did all the secretarial work from a converted dressing room at the Gateway and later from a small office with a single frosted glass window high in one wall. They used to say that was to prevent them looking at anything that was happening outside and complained they never had any time to do that anyway. Even now, with the bigger, more elaborate set-up in Glasgow, the administration, secretarial and logistical work is done from three small offices in the rehearsal building.

There were inevitable panics. The set for the drawing room of the Big House which was to feature in the first few episodes to be recorded was erected in the studio and found to be totally misconceived. It had been made gloomy and panelled, with stags' heads and ancient faded furniture, not what had been envisaged at all. Hasty changes were made and on the day the first episode was recorded, it had become a much brighter, more modern room.

The schedule in those days demanded that two episodes be recorded in the studio on two successive days each week. A few weeks into production word came from the week's director that his first episode had ended three minutes under its intended running time of twenty-four and a half minutes. Panic in the writers' room amongst the ad hoc script editing committee. By a fortunate chance, the next episode began with a two and a half minute

scene which had already been filmed on location. 'Okay', said Clarke Tait. 'Cut the film scene from tomorrow's episode and shove it on the end of this one. We'll have a new scene written overnight to make up the time lost in the second episode.' That was all very well, but what was the new scene to contain? It had to be something relevant to the story. It had to be played in one of the sets already available in the studio and, perhaps most important, it had to be played not only by actors already in the episode – otherwise extra fees would be payable – but by actors capable of learning a new scene and recording it with absolutely no rehearsal. In the event a scene was written which took place in Blair's Store between Eileen McCallum as Isabel Blair and Jimmy Chisholm as her son Jimmy, because those two could be trusted to be word perfect within half an hour of the new scene being handed to them in the morning. In the afternoon, when the scene was recorded, Eileen and Jimmy simply said, 'All right, tell us where to stand and we'll do it.' And they did. In one take. Yet more sighs of relief all round.

A further panic appeared from a totally different direction. There had been a change of mind. The network didn't want twenty-six episodes. They wanted thirty-two. Another six episodes had to be hastily concocted, actors' contracts had to be renegotiated, writers had to be recommissioned and film and studio crews reassigned. But the job was done.

In mid-February transmission began, not only of *Take the High Road* but also of Southern Television's soap opera, *Together*. Scottish Television was quietly confident about *Take the High Road* but they knew nothing of *Together*. It was a tense day at the Gateway when *Together* was transmitted for the first time. (*Taff's Acre*, from HTV, was to start transmission later). Rehearsals stopped and everyone gathered round a television set as

Some of the *Take the High Road* writers in the village hall set. Standing, William Andrew, Peter May, Bill Craig. Seated, Janice Hally, Tom Wright, producer Brian Mahoney, Michael Elder, Sue Glover.

Together began. When it was over there was a definite feeling of relief in the air. Surely *Take the High Road* would prove the more popular programme. For one thing, *Together* was set in a high-rise block of flats, the sort of background which Scottish Television had used for *High Living* more than ten years before. Was not this sort of background played out? And *Together* was transmitted live, which must have been an actor's nightmare. Although it contained some well-known and distinguished actors and actresses, the slow pace necessitated by live transmission where a fast cut from scene to scene is not often possible, made everyone at the Gateway that day believe that, although the method of recording *Take the High Road* was not ideal, it provided a tighter, faster-moving product. Also, *Together* was shot entirely in the studio. External filming was always, and remains, one of *Take the High Road*'s most valuable assets. Throughout its history it has probably used more film for location work than any other British soap opera.

Shortly after transmission started word came through that the network were commissioning a further series of twenty-four episodes. The battle had been won. *Take the High Road* had started its long career.

TWO

THE MAKING OF
TAKE THE HIGH ROAD

The pattern of making *Take the High Road* has changed considerably through the ten years since the programme started in 1980. The changes have taken place for two main reasons, firstly the development of new techniques in production, and secondly the growth in the number of episodes needed by the network. Starting from a series of twenty-six episodes (extended to thirty-two before the series had been completed) it has gradually grown until, in 1987, the requirement became 104 episodes a year, or a regular two a week. This has meant alterations in working practice, not only because of the logistics of actually making the programme, but also to allow actors and writers, technicians, crews and production staff time off to take a well-earned rest and recharge batteries. Making soap operas is a physically and mentally exhausting occupation.

Garnock Way, which had been transmitted in the Scottish Television area only, had gone out once a week throughout the year. It had been made for five years at Scottish Television's Gateway Studio in Edinburgh in batches of twenty-six episodes spread over three months. There had then been a three-month break before the next twenty-six went into produc-

tion. It was a regular and reasonably sedate way of making the programme, but one of the principal differences between *Garnock Way* and *Take the High Road* was the fact that *Garnock Way* contained practically no scenes shot on film outside the studio. There had been plans to upgrade *Garnock Way* to take in more location work, but these never came to fruition because the programme was cancelled to make way for *Take the High Road*. The fledgling soap opera followed *Garnock Way* into the Gateway.

The Gateway Studio is small, formed from the auditorium and stage of the old Gateway Theatre which, in its time, had been a variety theatre, a roller skating rink, a cinema and, under the ownership of the Church of Scotland, for over a decade in the 1950s and 1960s, contained Scotland's nearest approach to a national theatre it has achieved since the early days of the Citizen's Theatre in Glasgow. Scottish Television bought the Gateway from the Church of Scotland and, after extensive refurbishment, opened it as a television studio in December 1969. Perhaps because of its small size and number of staff there was a homely, friendly atmosphere about the place and since *Take the High Road*

A few 'weel-kent' faces celebrate the programme's 200th edition. At the front is director Paul Kimberley. Second from the left, executive producer Robert Love and extreme right, producer Brian Mahoney.

was virtually the only programme made in the studio, everything revolved round it.

From the outset *Take the High Road* was planned with a rough proportion of a third of each episode being shot outside. One of its main attractions is the Scottish scenery. The outside scenes are all shot around Loch Lomond, mainly in the picturesque little village of Luss which, since *Take the High Road* started, as discovered a huge increase in its tourist traffic. Always popular even before the series appeared on the television screen, bus parties now arrive in Luss throughout the summer from all parts of England, Scotland and Wales to see where the programme is made. At times it is very difficult to film scenes in the street because of the clicking of cameras unconnected with the programme!

The instant recognition of Loch Lomond as the setting for *Take the High Road* creates strange anomalies. Originally the imaginary village of Glendarroch was to be set somewhere near Oban, many miles to the north west, but this illusion was not sustainable against such a well-known background, so although Loch Lomond appears in almost every episode, it is always referred to as Loch Darroch and Ben Lomond in the background is Ben Darroch. Distances have become squashed. In the early episodes of *Take the High Road* the distance between Glendarroch and the nearest big town, Auchtarne, was twenty miles. It is now officially eight. Grace Lachlan had to be brought out of the Lachlan croft by helicopter in the second series when she had a heart attack because it was impossible to reach the croft by road. Now people drop in at all hours of the day for cups of tea.

There are, of course, other locations besides Luss. The outside of the Big House, for instance, is the Loch Lomond youth hostel, and there are various other locations just behind the youth hostel which save moving cameras and crews too far. *Take the High Road* works on a tight filming schedule and there is little time for packing, transporting and unpacking equipment. Inverdarroch's farm, Morag's croft and many of the external farming scenes are shot on a farm in Glen Fruin in the hills behind Luss.

In those early days, filming at Luss and working in the studio in Edinburgh, a geographical distance of something like seventy miles, did not present major problems because there were so few episodes being made and the pattern of making them was so flexible that problems of availability of actors and actresses rarely occurred. Since filming and studio work took place on different days of the week, it was only at rehearsals that artists might be missing if they were filming.

Technical facilities too have changed out of all recognition in the ten years of making *Take the High Road*. Looking back on those early days there was, by present day standards, a crudeness in the manner in which the programme was put together which would not happen now.

To begin with, there were no post-production facilities. This meant that once the videotape for transmission had been completed it could not be altered. What left the studio at the end of the recording day was the tape which the viewers later saw on their screens without any kind of addition, subtraction or alteration.

This put great pressure on work in the studio. Instead of recording a batch of scenes in the same set, thus saving enormously on the time and effort of lighting sets and turning cameras and sound booms round, each scene had to be recorded in what is known as story order. Every scene was recorded in the order in which it would eventually be seen, whether it was on film or in the studio. Scenes which had been filmed four weeks before at Luss had by now been processed and edited separ-

Left, it takes a lot of rain to raise the level of Loch Lomond to this height. The Aqua Sports office stands at the head of the landing stage which serves as the Glendarroch pier. This day the ferry could have tied up alongside the office!

Below, the actor's eye view of the camera crew prepared for inclement weather. At the right of the photograph director Jim McCann is flanked on his right by production assistant Margaret Hunter and on his left by stage manager Edith Hornall.

ately and were transferred from film on to the videotape at the appropriate points in the story.

A single episode was recorded in its entirety in the course of one day. Each week, two days were spent in the studio recording two episodes. The other three days were given over to rehearsal and filming.

After a dress rehearsal of the episode in the morning in the studio preparations began for recording it in the afternoon. As the videotape recording machine – VTR – was located at Scottish Television's Glasgow headquarters, the recording was sent over a British Telecom landline. The VTR machine was only available each recording day until six o'clock in the evening, after which it was required by News and Current Affairs, so each episode had to be recorded, complete and ready for transmission, in four hours.

At two o'clock the opening sequence of film for the titles was played through, the opening captions (the title caption, *Take the High Road*, and the writer's name) which were printed on cards and placed on caption stands for the cameras in the studio were superimposed on the film and then the first scene was cued in on the studio floor. The actors and actresses would play through the scene and the process would stop when a satisfactory recording of the scene had taken place. This was usually after several takes, because one of the curses of recording, particularly in those early days, was that although the actors might get it right, some technical problem would occur which necessitated recording the whole scene again. Sometimes the problem was the appearance of a microphone at the top of the shot. But much more frequently it was not the microphone itself but the shadow of the boom – the long arm that held it – which was often to be seen on the back wall of the set. This was a permanent headache for sound and lighting because the boom, of necessity, was always

between the lamps and the set they were lighting. The shout of 'Boom shadow!' spelt the death knell of many a scene during recording. However, the problems were not, and are not now, purely technical. Actors are human and forget lines and where they are supposed to be. On one occasion an actor stopped in the middle of recording with a slightly puzzled look on his face and said, 'I'm sorry. I don't think I'm in the right place. Where should I be?' And a voice from one of the sound operators said, 'Never mind. Just follow the boom shadow!'

But whether it was an actor drying or being in the wrong place, or whether it was a microphone or a boom shadow or even a camera getting into shot, if the recording had to stop, it meant going back to the beginning of the scene and rerecording the whole thing. In the case of the first scene of an episode it meant going right back to running the opening film and superimposing the captions all over again.

Once the scene was successfully recorded the cameras and the sound booms would move to the set where the next scene was to take place. The videotape on which the previous scene was recorded was wound back a little and the end of the previous scene was played in to the studio. Ten seconds before that scene ended the floor manager would start the countdown. 'Ten . . . nine . . . eight . . .' After 'one' he would cue the actors in the next scene and, if the timing was right, that scene would start recording at the exact point where the director wanted the previous scene to end. This was not always successful and many an actor was left at the end of a scene, seemingly for ages, with a frozen expression of surprise, horror, despair or joy on his or her face before the next scene got under way.

This method of production continued for the first seven years of *Take the High Road*'s

Stage manager Malcolm Morton stands in for a cameraman in the studio for this rather unusual publicity shot: no one can remember when the Lachlans were in the Glendarroch drawing room!

life. During those years, however, there were a few differences in other ways. For one thing the scripts became faster-moving. Looking back over the very first episodes now, it is surprising how slow the programme was. Fashions in television drama production change, and *Take the High Road* has changed with them. Each episode in the first series consisted of about eight scenes spread over the twenty-four and a half minutes of transmission time. This number has been gradually increased until now there is an average of twenty scenes per episode, which means that the scenes are shorter and sharper and the programme moves at a much quicker pace than it did in its early days. For another thing the number of episodes being made in each year gradually increased, so that the pressure in the studio grew. But administratively the programme is counted, not only by the total number of episodes, but also by the number of series made. Series do not necessarily mean the same as years. Sometimes two series were made in one year. Sometimes a series would run from one calendar year into the next. In 1990 the fourteenth series is being made, in spite of the fact that it is only the eleventh year of *Take the High Road*.

By late 1986, when the eleventh series was being made at the Gateway, the decision was finally taken that *Take the High Road* should become a regular twice weekly feature on the network. This was welcome news in many ways. It meant that the programme was now on an equal footing with other soap operas on the network. It had been difficult to maintain viewing figures when viewers were never sure if and when the programme was going to appear on their sets. An assurance of a regular twice weekly showing enabled the programme to build continuously on its viewing figures, although constant changes in transmission times among the different regions still make it very hard for viewers to trace the whereabouts

of the programme on their schedules. Often different regions are showing different episodes in the same week which tends to confuse viewers travelling between regions!

But the switch to 104 episodes a year meant fundamental changes in the way the programme was made. The whole process had to be rethought. The cast were summoned to a meeting in the rehearsal room at the Gateway one day and coffee and biscuits were provided. There was gloom and despondency. Many remembered the occasion more than seven years before when the axing of *Garnock Way* had been announced. There was glum acknowledgement at the end of each series that no one could be sure if the network controllers would ask Scottish Television to continue the programme for a further year. Was this to be the announcement of the end?

But the news this time was very different. It was simply that in order to accommodate the new number of episodes it had been decided to move the programme from the Gateway in Edinburgh to Studio A in Glasgow. There were, of course, groans from the half of the company who lived in Edinburgh, but there were cheers from the other half who lived in Glasgow and who had spent the previous seven years at the mercy of British Rail. Now the situation was to be reversed.

The move made sense. Studio A in Glasgow is much bigger. It was a purpose-built studio with enough height to light the show properly. (The Gateway's roof was low, always making lighting a problem.) It would hold six of *Take the High Road*'s sets at a time compared with only four at the Gateway. This would enable the programme to move faster and change its venues more frequently. There were also now to be post-production facilities, and these were all located in Glasgow. The old days of recording the scenes of an episode in story order were gone. From now on the scenes in each particular set would be recorded in a

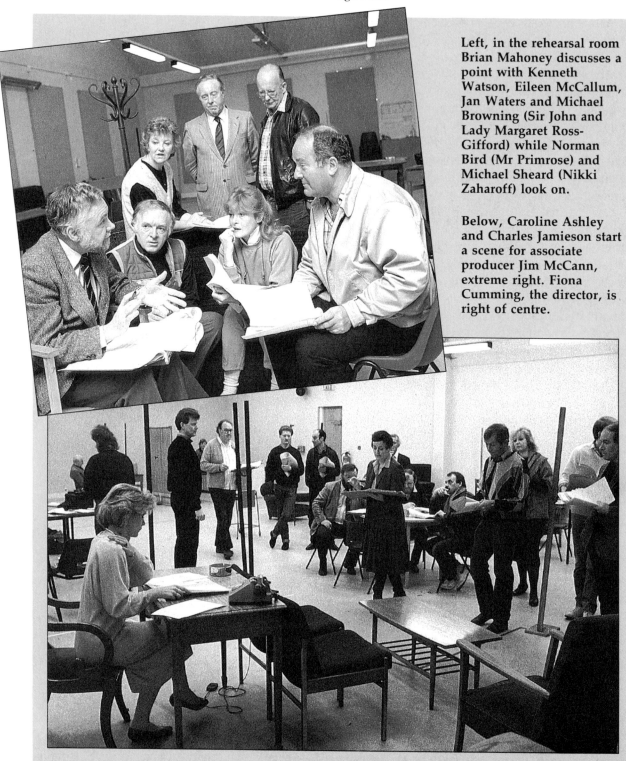

Left, in the rehearsal room Brian Mahoney discusses a point with Kenneth Watson, Eileen McCallum, Jan Waters and Michael Browning (Sir John and Lady Margaret Ross-Gifford) while Norman Bird (Mr Primrose) and Michael Sheard (Nikki Zaharoff) look on.

Below, Caroline Ashley and Charles Jamieson start a scene for associate producer Jim McCann, extreme right. Fiona Cumming, the director, is right of centre.

block, so saving time in studio turnaround.

But there was a definite disadvantage. In order to give staff, writers and actors a month's holiday in July and time off at Christmas and New Year – when many of the actors had long-standing pantomime and other Christmas stage show engagements – the schedule would have to be redrawn to allow the management to make three episodes a week instead of two. This, of course, vastly increased the workload and would have been impossible to undertake at the Gateway because now the logistics of getting actors and actresses to and from filming at Luss became critical. Glasgow to Luss is about thirty miles. An actor could leave the make-up room at Scottish Television at eight in the morning, be transported to Luss to film outdoor scenes for forthcoming episodes by nine, returned to Scottish Television by early afternoon and be in the studio to record scenes in the current episode or in the rehearsal room to rehearse scenes in next week's episodes. It was, indeed, a punishing schedule but it did turn out to be possible.

Just opposite their headquarters in the Cowcaddens in Glasgow, Scottish Television had bought an old building which had been garages and offices for a brewery. The floor space in here was used as the Scottish Television executive car park, but there was a warren of extra accommodation surrounding it, and in this area the management built a new rehearsal room, together with two green rooms for the *Take the High Road* cast. There were also new offices for *Take the High Road*'s administration and for the writers and script editors. Situated only two minutes walk from the main building and the studio itself, it was ideal for the purpose. Work was finished on this conversion in January 1987 in time for the company and staff to start making the first episodes of the new regular twice-weekly serial for the network.

THREE

IT HAPPENED IN GLENDARROCH

THE FERRY

There used to be a ferry between Glendarroch and Auchtarne, but it fell into disuse many years ago. While Maggie Ferguson ran her bus service between the village and the nearest big town there was no need to revive it. But when Maggie married Sorry Watson and went to live in Shetland with him, the bus service stopped and it was very difficult to get to Auchtarne from Glendarroch except by the road round the head of the loch by the postbus – and it only made the journey once a day in each direction – or by taxi which was prohibitively expensive. The village became so cut off from the outside world that Jimmy Blair suggested reviving the ferry and Sorry Watson, perhaps because he had been instrumental in depriving the people of their bus, agreed to finance it. He also got the licence from the Education Authority to carry the schoolchildren from Glendarroch to the secondary school in Auchtarne, which made the ferry a viable proposition.

The ferry was run first by Jimmy Blair, then for a time by Eddie Ramsay and after he left the area, by Brian Blair who, with Sorry's assistance, developed it into something a little bigger than a simple ferry. The old boat became unseaworthy and Sorry invested in a bigger, newer boat which in summer could also take passengers on cruises round the loch.

For most people their first sight of Glendarroch was from the ferry as they sailed across from Auchtarne and for many years it was an integral part of the life of the village.

On the night of the Great Storm Jimmy brought Dr Wallace across on the ferry in appalling conditions to attend to Fraser Ramsay, trapped and seriously injured by a fallen tree.

Sheila Ramsay's cousin, Jennifer, stole the ferry when it was discovered she had kidnapped the baby she said was hers.

Jimmy Blair and Marion Cochrane, in the ferry, found an overturned fishing boat and the body of the fisherman in the middle of the loch.

After Brian Blair departed for the south it was hard to find someone willing and capable of running the ferry. The last person to operate it was Scott Logan. But he lived in Auchtarne, which meant he had to bring the boat over for the first run and the schoolchildren due to leave Glendarroch at eight o'clock in the morning – an impossibly early start.

Right, spring comes reluctantly and Ben Darroch's head is still white.

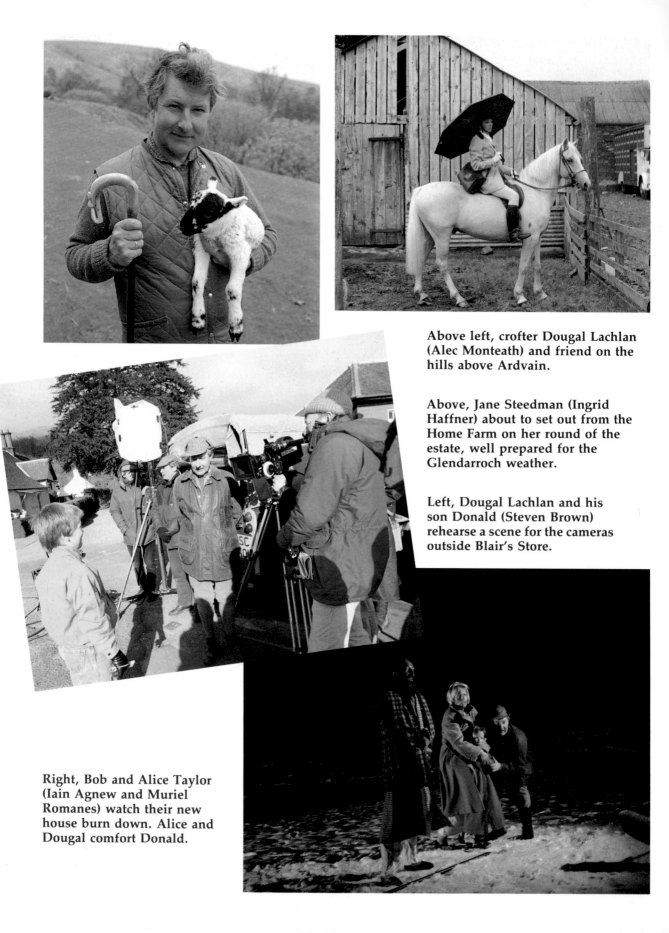

Above left, crofter Dougal Lachlan (Alec Monteath) and friend on the hills above Ardvain.

Above, Jane Steedman (Ingrid Haffner) about to set out from the Home Farm on her round of the estate, well prepared for the Glendarroch weather.

Left, Dougal Lachlan and his son Donald (Steven Brown) rehearse a scene for the cameras outside Blair's Store.

Right, Bob and Alice Taylor (Iain Agnew and Muriel Romanes) watch their new house burn down. Alice and Dougal comfort Donald.

Left, Harry Shaw, the pop star Vincent, and his wife Sally (Laurie McNicol and Judith Sweeney) at Letir-Falloch. Note the rare smile on the face of factor Davie Sneddon (Derek Lord).

Below, Ruari Galbraith (Charles Jamieson) comforts Fiona Cunningham (Caroline Ashley) during the birth of their son, David. That is the cameraman beyond the bed, not the anaesthetist!

Below, Morag Steward (Jeannie Fisher) follows Effie McInnes (Mary Riggans) along a road near Glendarroch.

The boat used as Glendarroch's first ferry became unseaworthy so Scottish Television were forced to write in a reason for a change. This is the second ferry and the camera crew are setting up a shot from the new boat.

Left, high summer, and the Ben, its white head briefly gone, continues to guard Loch Darroch.

By then the road to Auchtarne was being improved, more people had cars and the need for the ferry began to wane. Eventually it became too expensive to maintain the boat for the diminishing returns and the ferry again passed into oblivion.

VISIONS OF KATRINA

Bob Taylor, the water bailiff and Archie Menzies, the estate handyman, browsing one day through a copy of *The Crofter and Farmer*, remarked on the number of advertisements there were for farmers looking for wives. Their conversation turned to wondering if it mightn't be a good idea for Dougal Lachlan seeing he was making little progress with Morag Stewart at the time. From there it was a simple step for Bob and Archie to draft the sort of advertisement that might elicit a reply. The final wording bore no relation to Dougal at all: *Artistic crofter with special interest in the ballet seeks like-minded soul mate . . .*

Archie typed it out on Lorna Seton's typewriter in the estate office. He even typed an envelope addressed to *The Crofter and Farmer*, intending to show it to Dougal as a joke. But Archie left the envelope with the advertisement in it on Lorna's desk and Lorna, not knowing what it was, posted it.

It would still be all right, thought Archie and Bob: the paper would never publish it because they hadn't enclosed the money. But when *The Crofter and Farmer* rang the office about the advertisement Lorna promised the bill would be paid and the advertisement duly appeared. Dougal saw the advertisement and noticed to his horror his own name and address at the end of it.

Then the replies began to come in, dozens of them, and Dougal's horror began to turn to a kind of self-satisfaction as he went through them. Obviously he was attractive to women,

the Casanova of Glendarroch, although the other crofters and a highly indignant Morag scoffed at him. Eventually, as Dougal became more and more engrossed in the replies Archie and Bob had to confess they were responsible. But by that time Dougal was so taken with the idea he forgave them and actually thanked them for putting the advertisement in for him.

By this time one reply had led Dougal into a correspondence. It started with a letter from someone called Katrina who gave her address simply as care of the post office, Auchtarne. Dougal wrote back and she replied. The letters came almost daily and Fergus Jamieson, the postman, was fed up delivering them.

Dougal gave Katrina details of the lambing and the dipping and the shearing to which she responded with frank and deep interest and reading between the lines Dougal suspected she was an excellent cook and a careful and economical housekeeper. He found himself more and more attracted to the thought of Katrina, though she shyly and persistently refused to meet him.

He tried to intercept her at the Auchtarne post office when she collected his replies, and nearly got arrested when the postmistress thought he was loitering with intent. He asked everyone if they knew a Katrina. Some did. Robert Forsyth knew a Katrina in Auchtarne but she was over eighty years old and unlikely to consider the proposal of marriage Dougal was now contemplating. Morag remembered a Katrina at school but refused to divulge her last name.

At last after many importunities on Dougal's part, Katrina wrote that she could no longer resist the thought of meeting him, and if he cared to come to the Auchtarne Arms and give her dinner the following night, she would be there. Dougal, highly excited at the prospect, and dressed in his Sunday best, turned up at the hotel to find – Morag Stewart.

Above, Marion Cochrane (Lizzie Radford) and Jimmy Blair (Jimmy Chisholm) have just found the body of a man drowned in a boating accident. They are using the first Glendarroch ferry.

Right, Dougal Lachlan (Alec Monteath) does not look particularly pleased at receiving the attentions of Morag Stewart (Jeannie Fisher).

THE SPONSORED SWIM

Glendarroch's need of a lifeboat became more urgent after Jimmy Blair and Marion Cochrane found the body of a fisherman in the loch. There were accidents every year, some of them fatal, but this discovery by two young people on their own brought it home as nothing else had done how dangerous the loch was to the inexperienced and the venturesome. With the development of fishing and boating for tourists these accidents were likely to increase. The ferry was too slow to use as a lifeboat: what was needed was a fast inflatable such as the inshore rescue boats used by the Royal National Lifeboat Institution. But these were expensive. Nevertheless the village determined to raise the money, and when Sorry Watson offered to match them pound for pound, enthusiasm and determination grew.

Events were planned. One, a concert in the village hall, was organised by Mrs Mack, the minister's housekeeper. The highlight, a duet sung by Mr Murdoch, the clerk to the Kirk Session, and Mrs Mack herself was a disaster – as was the concert. But money was raised – £200 which when doubled by Sorry Watson was £400 for the lifeboat fund.

The biggest event of the year was a sponsored swim – a race on the loch over a measured distance – for all comers including the stars of the Auchtarne High School Swimming Club. Everybody was invited to sponsor their favourites.

Organisation on the day was meticulous – police and medical facilities were there – as well as boats on the loch to follow the swimmers and assist any who got into difficulties.

Even so, there was a near disaster. The swim took place, but when it was over and the roll call was read, one swimmer was missing. Carol Mackay from the High School had not returned. Boats and rescuers searched the loch without success. There were murmurs that the lifeboat was proving too costly in human lives even before it was bought.

Darkness fell and still Carol was not found. Gloom settled over the village. The event that had raised hopes high had become a village tragedy. Perhaps the whole idea of a lifeboat should be abandoned.

But that evening Carol was discovered – at home – cold, wet and embarrassed, so embarrassed it took some time to learn her story. When she dived off the pier at the start of the race she had lost her costume. She tried to recover it but the water was too deep. So she had hidden under the pier, shivering and miserable, until darkness fell and everyone had disappeared, before creeping home unseen.

The sponsored swim had turned out to be a great success after all, but only at the last minute.

THE SHINTY MATCH

Archie Menzies, as chairman of the lifeboat appeal committee, took his duties very seriously. Some of his ideas for raising money were potentially excellent, like the sponsored swim. Others were potentially disastrous, like the shinty match.

Discussing with Bob Taylor one day the merits of shinty as a game, Archie had the idea of arranging a match between a Glendarroch team and a select team from Auchtarne. No one favoured this idea. Hardly any of the men had played shinty before, and those who had were now too old to play it again. But Archie was determined. He appointed himself coach and general manager of a Glendarroch team. He organised a willing team from Auchtarne to play against it. Auchtarne had an interest in a lifeboat on the

Left, Carol Mackay (Teri Lally) freezing in Loch Lomond in October as she prepares to take part in the sponsored swim.

Peter May, writer of the sponsored swim episode, volunteered to take part to prove swimming in Loch Lomond wasn't as bad as it was made out. It was. Afterwards he was glad of a cup of coffee.

Jimmy Blair (Jimmy Chisholm), Eddie Ramsay (Robin Cameron), Peter Craig (Jay Smith), Bob Taylor (Iain Agnew) and Inverdarroch (John Stahl) carry a triumphant Morag Stewart (Jeannie Fisher) from the shinty field.

loch as well. He had more difficulty in raising a willing team from Glendarroch. Eventually Archie scratched together enough players and a few reserves. Bob Taylor, Brian Blair, Ken Calder, Eddie Ramsay, Jimmy Blair, Dougal Lachlan and Inverdarroch were finally persuaded.

Morag Stewart watched their first practice session and was appalled. She knew something about shinty; she had been an avid follower of the game and she had played hockey at the Auchtarne High School. She wanted to be included in the team. She couldn't be any worse than most of those who were playing, she said. Archie just laughed and absolutely forbade it. The other members of the team were little better. But the women of the village were on Morag's side, especially when they heard just how bad the men were likely to be. The women who had been asked to make the strips for the match announced they were on strike unless Morag was included in the team. Archie was forced in the end to include her – as the last reserve – and the strips were completed.

Word got to Auchtarne about how awful the opposition was going to be and Archie, an inveterate gambler, took bets that Glendarroch wouldn't even score a single hail against them.

The day of the match arrived and the Auchtarne team turned up. There was alarm and despondency when it was discovered that in the team was Killer McGurk who had played in the final of the Camanachd Cup and had a reputation for brute strength second to none.

The match started and Killer McGurk's reputation was justified. Man after man in the Glendarroch team retired with an injury until all the reserves had been used – except Morag. With great reluctance, Archie sent Morag on.

Morag had a strange effect on Killer McGurk. For some reason he was terrified of her and when she contemptuously called him 'Wee Tumshie' McGurk he spent the rest of the game trying to hide from her – so much so that Morag scored a hail against Auchtarne. Although Glendarroch failed to win the match, Morag's single hail allowed Archie to clean up a lot on the book he had made at Auchtarne and the match raised a lot of money for the lifeboat fund. As for Morag, she was chaired off the field by the rest of the Glendarroch team as though they had actually won the game.

POACHING FISH

Bob Taylor, the water bailiff, had a fine new scheme to attract more fishing on the Glendarroch estate and consequently acquire more cash from fishing permits. He stocked the Nor' Loch, one of the high lochs, with a large and valuable crop of young trout to develop there before transferring them to Loch Darroch for the fishing season.

They did well until one day, while measuring them for development, Bob was accosted by Davie Sneddon, the unpopular factor of Letir-Falloch, the neighbouring estate. When Bob told him about his scheme, Sneddon said Nor' Loch was on Letir-Falloch land and if he took fish from it he'd have him up for poaching. Bob told him not to be ridiculous. The Nor' Loch was on Glendarroch land and always had been. But Sneddon was adamant. The Nor' Loch belonged to Letir-Falloch and he repeated his warning.

Bob was worried. Sneddon seemed so sure, but although he and the Lady Laird, Elizabeth Cunningham, checked and doubled checked, it seemed perfectly clear that the Nor' Loch was on Glendarroch land.

At this time Mr McPherson, the minister, was researching an article about the old days in Glendarroch which he was intending to write for *Scottish Life*. This was to be in greater depth than the short one he had recently had published in *Church and Nation*. While studying some old maps of Glendarroch Archie had unearthed for him in the Big House attic, he discovered that over many hundreds of years the course of the burn which fed the Nor' Loch had changed, that the Nor' Loch had therefore been on Letir-Falloch land and, worse, that nothing had ever been done to change it.

Bob went to Sneddon, apologised for encroaching on Letir-Falloch land and said he would remove the fish to complete their development elsewhere. Sneddon refused to allow such a thing. How could Bob tell which were his fish and which were fish already in The Nor' Loch? Any attempt to remove the fish would be regarded as poaching, said Sneddon, and would mean police action.

This caused much indignation in the village and a plot was hatched to remove the fish without Sneddon's knowledge and relocate them in a loch indisputably on Glendarroch land.

One of the main problems in mounting the operation was how to get the key to the padlock on the gate which closed the track to the Nor' Loch. Sneddon kept this well guarded. It was Effie McInnes, housekeeping at Letir-Falloch at the time, who got hold of the key for the conspirators. The gate was unlocked and a motley collection of vans, cars and handcarts was assembled for the operation at the loch.

Sneddon got wind of it and summoned Sergeant Murray and Constable McPhee. But Archie, using a borrowed fish and chip van as what he described as a red herring, drew Sneddon and the police away from the action, while the entire village removed the fish from the loch in a variety of strange receptacles. Sneddon was thwarted, but Effie McInnes lost her job as housekeeper for her part in the plot.

THE HORSE RACE

After Fiona Cunningham fell off her horse knocking herself unconscious it took her a long time to recover mentally. However, she got better at last and began to ride again with increasing confidence. Then one day she met Sneddon at the market.

His snide remarks about her falling off her horse, about spending time in the funny farm and his suggestion that she should take a few more riding lessons finally goaded Fiona into arguing instead of ignoring him. The upshot was that Sneddon suggested they revive the old Glendarroch-Letir-Falloch horse race, in abeyance for many years, in which a rider from each estate raced the other, the winner receiving the loser's horse as a prize. Fiona accepted and Sneddon was confident he was on to a good thing. Then one day he secretly watched Fiona practising and realised she was a much better rider than he was himself. This worried him as he would have to use one of his boss Harry Shaw's horses for the race. If he lost it to Fiona it would be difficult to explain away.

But then Fiona became pregnant and riding in this race was medically inadvisable. With some embarrassment she asked for a postponement. Sneddon was quite agreeable so long as she gave him the horse she would have ridden if the race had taken place. This Fiona angrily refused to do and the race was on again.

It was Archie who organised a way of winning the race without Fiona playing any dangerous part in it. A ringer, a substitute, would be used. Not so much a substitute horse, but a substitute rider. The prescribed course for the race split in two – a short, very difficult course and a longer much more straightforward one. It was obvious that Sneddon, a less skilled rider, would take the long straight course, so if Fiona took the short

Left, preparing for the Glendarroch horse race. Mrs Mack knows as little about horses as she does about anything else, so Gwyneth Guthrie is wearing the most sensible hat she has ever worn in the programme.

Below, Mrs Mack, having been deposited by her horse in a thicket of brambles, emerges with her dignity somewhat battered – at least the other members of the cast seem to think so.

one someone could substitute for her on a different horse as soon as she was out of sight of Sneddon. The substitute could then take the horse past the two stewards appointed to watch the race, while the real horse was transported by horsebox to a point near the finishing line. There Fiona would remount and gallop the last hundred yards or so, thereby, everyone hoped, winning the race for Glendarroch.

Fiona, thinking Sneddon might well renege on giving her his horse if and when he lost, invited Harry Shaw to witness the race. Harry was not best pleased when he heard the terms.

On the day of the race the substitutes were in place. Carol Mackay and Sheila Ramsay were to take the substitute horse past the stewards whom Archie would have nobbled by plying them with whisky. All went smoothly until Mrs Mack suddenly insisted on substituting for one of the substitutes and managed to mount the horse. Thereupon the horse bolted with her, raced past the waiting Fiona and on through the winning post before stopping and throwing Mrs Mack into a bed of nettles.

Sneddon arrived a few minutes later, furious to discover the trick that had been played on him. But he could do nothing about it when Harry Shaw declared the race a draw and Sneddon stalked off with the laughter of the participants and spectators, including Harry Shaw, ringing in his ears.

A TRIP TO VENICE

Sorry Watson put up a ticket to Venice as the first prize in a raffle in aid of the lifeboat fund. Mrs Mack was desperately keen to win as she dearly wished to visit this city of history and culture. She read up about Venice in the minister's encyclopaedia and gazetteer and began to rhapsodise about it to everybody she met and even got to the stage of promising the people of the village a lecture on her trip in the village hall after she got back.

Archie Menzies was not so interested in the first prize as he was in the second, a very large bottle of whisky.

But when it came to the draw Archie won the trip to Venice and Mr Murdoch won the bottle of whisky. Mrs Mack won nothing at all.

No one was happy, particularly Mrs Mack, who said she had never wanted to go to Venice anyway, that the place was sinking and she wouldn't have wanted it to do that while she was there, that the canals were nothing more than open sewers and the heat would have been unbearable.

Then the horse trading started. Archie had already been warned by Lorna that the ticket involved travelling to Venice by air and that flying in that area could be extremely dangerous. Archie had genuinely never wanted to go to Venice anyway. With his eye on Murdoch's prize he offered to swap with him. Since Mrs Mack had already been criticising Mr Murdoch heavily for winning the whisky, telling him how bad it would be for his constitution and making many other similar remarks till his life was a misery, Mr Murdoch agreed to swop with Archie. This only made matters worse with Mrs Mack who thought it disgraceful that he should get the chance of a real cultural visit at the cost of a bottle of whisky, that he was totally incapable of appreciating the finer points of the trip and that if he had any spirit of Christian charity he would pass it on to her.

Eventually her tactics worked and in order to get peace, Mr Murdoch gave her the ticket. Satisfied, and with the canals apparently returned to a more sanitary condition, Mrs Mack went off to Venice.

She was even more impossible than usual

when she got home, talking in glowing terms of the Rialto and the Grand Canal and the glories of the Doge's Palace and St Mark's Square and of a certain Giovanni Luigi Rossini who had been their guide and with whom she had established a bond of cultural sympathy. She arranged to give her lecture on her experiences and even asked the Ross-Giffords, who had only just bought the estate, to attend. Lady Margaret had not the slightest intention of doing so, but Sir John thought it would be a good opportunity to become involved in village affairs and insisted that they went together.

Mrs Mack was to show the slides she had taken on the trip, but there was a delay in getting them back from the chemist in Auchtarne and they only arrived a minute or two before the lecture was due to take place.

The lecture began. The slides were awful. They were out of focus, fogged and generally indistinguishable – except for one of a hand-some, well-built young Italian with a flashing smile. This was Giovanni Luigi Rossini, the guide on the trip, and when his face and figure suddenly appeared on the screen and Mrs Mack broke down and was unable to continue, it was obvious that the bond of cultural sympathy between them had been considerably more than that – to her, at least.

Lady Margaret stepped into the breach and finished the lecture for her. Having been to Venice many times in the past she knew better than Mrs Mack the history and culture of the city, and the lecture that had been heading for disaster under Mrs Mack's control or lack of it, suddenly became full of interest, and the day was saved.

THE BOAT

Fergus Jamieson, the postman, had always wanted a boat. He longed to be able to row out into the loch on a sunny day and fall asleep to the sound of the water lapping against the hull, so when he found an old boat for sale in a yard in Auchtarne he bought it. He told Archie what he had done, that the boat needed a little work on it and would Archie be interested in a half share? Archie went to see the boat, saw the wrong one – in much better condition than Fergus's – and agreed to go halves with him.

It was only then that Archie discovered he had estimated on the wrong boat, that it would cost a great deal more to make Fergus's boat seaworthy, if it were possible at all, and they simply hadn't the money to do it. In desperation to raise more money they persuaded Mr Murdoch that it was a good finanical proposition and he agreed to come in with them for a third share.

But there still wasn't enough money. Archie had another brainwave. Timeshare on a boat. He managed to sell the idea to Mark Ritchie, the owner-editor of *The Auchtarne Herald*. Mark was a keen fisherman and in return for a hundred pounds – which would perhaps make the boat seaworthy – he could get the use of the boat for fishing whenever he wanted it. It seemed to Mark to be too good a chance to miss, so, having inspected the boat on which Archie had put in some cosmetic work and which now looked reasonable on the surface, he paid up.

Archie suggested salmon fishing to Fergus and Mr Murdoch. They could catch salmon from the boat in the loch and sell them to the kitchen at the Auchtarne Arms, no questions asked, and recoup some of their losses. There was some doubt about whether salmon in the loch were private property or not. Mr Murdoch, as the expert in poaching, believed they were not, so an inaugural trip was organised and Fergus, Archie, Mr Murdoch and Mark Ritchie set off one morning with the rods and the gear, ready for a fine day's fishing on the loch.

They caught six fish too, a good haul. And then the boat began to take in water. They discovered they didn't have a baler. The engine wouldn't restart, and when they tried to row home, they found that one of the rowlocks was missing and they could only proceed in circles.

It was a cold night on the loch and by the morning they were frozen, exhausted from constantly trying to keep the level of the water in the boat down and Mark Ritchie at least was extremely angry. There was consternation ashore too when it was discovered that the four were missing.

They were eventually traced by Scott Logan in the Glendarroch-Auchtarne ferry with Sergeant Murray on board. As it approached, hasty attempts were made to remove the evidence of fishing, much to Mark Ritchie's fury as he had thought everything was above board and, as a responsible member of the community, he did not appreciate being involved in illegal activity, however innocently.

The boat was by now low in the water, as the few articles on board they could use for baling barely allowed them to keep pace with the inflow. Scott Logan had the four castaways brought aboard and took the boat in tow. Halfway back, though, the boat became totally waterlogged and Scott Logan insisted they cut the towline. Sergeant Murray watched the boat sink, carrying Fergus's dreams to the bottom of the loch as well as all the evidence of illegal poaching – except for the two salmon Archie had managed to stuff down his trouser legs.

CLAIRE'S WEDDING

Inverdarroch's happiness meant so much to Morag Stewart that she threw herself gladly into the preparations for his wedding with Claire Millar, the district nurse. She agreed at once to be bridesmaid when the old friend Claire had asked accepted a nursing job in America and had to decline. She also offered to make the wedding dress.

Claire had hoped Michael Ross would perform the ceremony, but he thought Mr Parker, as minister of the parish, ought to be asked. This Inverdarroch refused to contemplate, having little time for Mr Parker. Eventually the much loved Mr McPherson was persuaded to come out of retirement and marry them. Mr Parker was not pleased.

But who was to give Claire away? It was only on the night before the ceremony that Claire realised there was no obvious candidate. Both her parents were dead and she had no near relations. To choose one of the local people might cause friction amongst the others, for Claire was very popular in the village. Someone suggested Sir John, but he and Claire both agreed that it wasn't right since he hardly knew her and she would not feel comfortable walking down the aisle on the arm of a stranger. But he did offer his car and Archie as chauffeur to get her to the church. But there was still no one to escort her, and she was to be married next day. Claire said she didn't mind. If the worst came to the worst she would walk down the aisle by herself. Mr McPherson reluctantly agreed, though he was not sure if that was a good idea.

Next day Claire and Morag arrived at the church in Sir John's car. Archie parked it and went into the church. Claire and Morag were left alone outside and at that point Claire took fright. She couldn't face walking down the aisle on her own. Perhaps the marriage was a mistake. Perhaps it wasn't meant . . . Morag tried to comfort her, offering to go into the church and get Archie out again – he could take her down the aisle. But Claire couldn't allow that. He had been seen arriving. To drag him out again would look very strange.

Smiles from the bride and groom on the day that Claire Millar (Julie Miller) and Inverdarroch (John Stahl) were married by Mr McPherson. But clouds were already gathering on the horizon.

Members of the cast often give up a great deal of their free time to charity work. Here Caroline Ashley and Alec Monteath, accompanied by John Carmichael on the accordion, entertain the residents of an old people's home.

It was at that moment Davie Sneddon passed by. Claire, on impulse, ran to him and asked if he would escort her to her wedding with Inverdarroch. He agreed. Morag protested in vain. Claire overruled her and with Sneddon by her side walked into the church. No one was more astonished and mortified than Inverdarroch and Hamish McNeil, his best man, to see the bride appear on the arm of the man who for years had taunted and sneered at Inverdarroch.

So shocked and angry was Inverdarroch that it was a surprise to no one that later, at the reception, there was a stand up fight between him and Sneddon. It was not a good omen for his future with Claire.

FOUR

THE CHARACTERS
AND WHO PLAY THEM

Emma Aitken was born in Harrogate, the daughter of Gladys Aitken and her first husband, George. When Gladys was working night and day to repay the debts left by her husband, Emma got involved with a gang of car thieves, even getting to the fringe of the drug scene. As Gladys in her present circumstances was not able to look after Emma, she had reluctantly to agree to her being taken into care. At the age of eighteen Emma had to leave the home and might well have slipped back into the life of crime had she not heard that her mother was about to remarry. She came to Glendarroch to trace her and has remained there ever since.

Amanda Whitehead who plays the volatile Emma Aitken was born in Oldham and educated at Royton and Crompton Comprehensive School, the Grange Arts Centre in Oldham and the Royal Scottish Academy of Music and Drama. Since then she has worked at the Lyceum Theatre in Edinburgh, at Oldham Coliseum Theatre and with the Atlas Theatre Company appearing at the Traverse Theatre in Edinburgh and at Mayfest in Glasgow. As a change from Emma Aitken she played the Good Fairy in Cavalcade Theatre Company's production of *Snow White* last Christmas. Amanda lists her hobbies as the

theatre, the cinema, going out for tasty meals and having fun.

Gladys Aitken is an Englishwoman who married George Aitken, a Scotsman born in Drumchinan, the neighbouring town to Auchtarne and moved south to run a newsagent's/tobacconist's in Harrogate. Her husband died a few years after the marriage, leaving Gladys with enormous debts. She worked hard to repay them and succeeded. Her husband had subscribed to a weekly copy of *The Auchtarne Herald* and Gladys had never got round to cancelling it. In fact she found some comfort in reading about the area of Scotland her husband had come from and in one edition she read an article written by Sheila Ramsay describing the life of Dougal Lachlan, a crofter on the Glendarroch estate. On an impulse Gladys wrote to Dougal and a correspondence arose, culminating in an invitation from Dougal to visit the croft. This Gladys did, unaware that the main reason for Dougal issuing the invitation was that he believed Gladys's original letter was a trick being played on him by Hamish McNeil, Archie Menzies and Bob Taylor and he was simply going along with it. When Gladys found out the real reason for his invitation she was very distressed and left immediately, to

Right, Dougal Lachlan (Alec Monteath) and Gladys Aitken (Ginni Barlow) got married at a registry office in Glasgow. In front of the happy couple are Alice Taylor (Barbara Rafferty), Donald Lachlan (Steven Brown) and Grace Lachlan (Marjorie Thomson).

Left, while her mother was getting married in Glasgow, Emma Aitken (Amanda Whitehead) turned up from Harrogate and has remained in Glendarroch ever since. Amanda can't remember now whether the ladder in her tights was intentional or not, but reckons that it must have been or someone would have spotted it!

return some time later at Dougal's earnest entreaty, and marry him.

Ginni Barlow, who plays Gladys Aitken, was born in Dumbarton and educated at Knoxland Primary School and Dumbarton Academy, before going for a while to the Glasgow School of Art and then transferring to the Royal Scottish Academy of Music and Drama. She has worked in the theatre all over Scotland and England and appeared at the Shaftesbury Theatre in London for two years with the Theatre of Comedy. She was in Scottish Television's previous soap opera, *Garnock Way* for its whole run, playing the landlady of the local pub. She lists amongst her hobbies oil painting, walking, singing and listening to classical music.

Nan Anderson is one of the Glendarroch worthies. She took on the job of housekeeper at Letir-Falloch for Davie Sneddon after Mrs Russell gave up the job. She was the ideal person to do it, because all Sneddon's insults and rudeness slide off her like water off a duck's back. She tends to smother him with motherliness and never believes that he is capable of any ill deed or nasty thought.

Marjorie Dalziel, who plays Mrs Anderson, was educated at St Margaret's in Edinburgh and Laurelbank, Glasgow and then trained at the George Dalziel Drama Studios in Glasgow. She first broadcast from Blythswood Square and was one of the cast of *The McFlannels*, perhaps the greatest Scottish radio series of all time. She has appeared in many television and radio series since, including *Dr Finlay's Casebook, Sunset Song, The White Bird Passes* and was for a long time a regular in *Garnock Way*. She was a founder member of The Edinburgh Gateway Company and has worked at the Glasgow Citizen's. For four years she was with Bertha Waddell's Children's Theatre Company and was on the staff of the Glasgow Drama College for five years. Marjorie has a son who is one of the leading Earth scientists in the United States and she is married to Dougal Spencer. They live in a small village near Stirling where she produces plays for her local drama club. Her hobbies are travel, painting, crosswords, playing the piano, dancing and reading.

Colin Begg is the new local vet, the fourth to have practised in Glendarroch. He is single and there was a time when there seemed to be a likelihood that he and Morag Stewart might get married, but nothing came of it.

Kern Falconer plays the part.

Brian Blair, the husband of Isabel Blair, served ten years of a life sentence for murdering a waitress at the Auchtarne Arms. At the time, Isabel had rejected him, blaming him for the fact that her second pregnancy had to be terminated by a hysterectomy. Because of Isabel's rejection Brian formed a liaison with the waitress who threatened to blackmail him by telling Isabel of their affair. Brian was fearful of Isabel's mental condition and, to save her, he murdered the girl and said nothing at his trial about the circumstances. The Blair temper has always been evident in Brian, and when he was released on licence, he lived under the constant threat of being recalled to serve the remainder of his sentence at the slightest sign of trouble, real or imagined. Because he was released on licence it was difficult for him to find any kind of gainful employment in Glendarroch. Eventually he went to London to help his sister-in-law, Helen, look after her younger daughter, Sandra, who had got caught up in the drugs scene. Brian found that, working voluntarily at the rehabilitation centre Sandra attended, he was accepted by the inmates when they heard of his past as an anti-establishment figure and he was able to relate to them and

Brian and Isabel Blair (Kenneth Watson and Eileen McCallum) with the ferry behind them. In spite of the sunny smiles the relationship, one of the most enduring in Glendarroch, was not to last for very much longer.

help them in a really meaningful way. When he was offered a full-time, paid job at the centre he accepted it and asked Isabel to come south to join him. But Isabel refused to leave Glendarroch, so the two, who had been childhood sweethearts, drifted apart.

Brian Blair is played by Kenneth Watson who trained at the Royal Academy of Dramatic Art and has worked with theatre companies as far apart as Aberdeen and Colchester. He has appeared in many feature films and has a long list of television credits. He lives in London with his wife, Joan, and they have a son and a daughter.

David Blair, the younger brother of Brian, was the brainier of the two. He took a degree in biochemistry at Glasgow University. He and his wife, Helen, have two daughters and they are now based in London, although David spends a lot of his time abroad, especially in the Gulf States. David never believed that his brother had committed the murder for which he served a life sentence. He felt that much evidence had not come out at the trial, and Brian's repeated assurances that he was guilty only seemed to convince David that he was innocent.

Derek Anders plays David Blair.

Helen Blair, David Blair's wife is English and hasn't got much time for her relations in Glendarroch. She has only appeared there on rare occasions. Her marriage to David Blair has had its ups and downs through the years, mainly because David spends so much time away from home.

Bridget Biagi plays Helen.

Isabel Blair was born and bred in Glendarroch. She married her childhood sweetheart, Brian Blair, whose parents ran the post office-cum

general store and when his parents died Brian and she took it over. She ran the store and the post office and looked after her son, Jimmy, during his formative years entirely on her own, due to Brian's absence in jail, and on Brian's release on licence she found it difficult to adjust to his return and to cope with his moods of depression. When he went south to help look after his niece, Isabel began to search for something more meaningful to do with her life and, discovering that their local regional councillor was not doing his job properly, she stood in opposition to him at the local council election. Due to some dirty work on the part of Robert Watt, the sitting councillor, she failed to gain the seat by a handful of votes and when Watt was arrested for not declaring his interests in businesses seeking council contracts, Isabel was asked to stand at the by-election. She declined.

In real life Eileen McCallum, who plays Isabel Blair, has been married for thirty years to Edinburgh art dealer Tom Fidelo, who is American. They have four children, Mark, Neal, Sarah and Tim. Eileen is the daughter of Gordon McCallum who was known for many years to a generation of children as the author of the ever popular Children's Hour radio series *Down at the Mains*. She was educated at Hutcheson's Girls Grammar School in Glasgow, Glasgow University where she obtained an M.A. degree in 1956 and the Royal Scottish Academy of Music and Drama where she won the gold medal in 1959. She began her broadcasting career in Children's Hour at the age of twelve with the legendary Kathleen Garscadden alongside such other young women as Gwyneth Guthrie (Mrs Mack) and Mary Riggans (Effie McInnes).

Jimmy Blair was the son of Brian and Isabel. During the period of his father's imprisonment Jimmy was the main support of his mother, helping her in the shop. He formed an early friendship with Fiona Cunningham, the daughter of the Lady Laird, and together they started an Aquasports business which, under the guidance of Sorry Watson, was reasonably successful but did not last. Jimmy, again with Sorry Watson's backing, revived the long-defunct Glendarroch–Auchtarne ferry when Maggie Ferguson married Sorry Watson, went to live in Shetland and left Glendarroch without a bus service. Jimmy eventually fell in love with Sally Shaw, the wife of Harry Shaw, better known as the pop star Vincent, and when she left him to return to her husband who had had a car accident in America during a tour there, Jimmy, fed up with his parents' disapproval of the affair, left Glendarroch. He found work in a chandler's in Glasgow where one day he was severely beaten up by a gang of thugs whom he had surprised trying to rob the place. He died in hospital a few weeks later.

Jimmy Chisholm, who played Jimmy Blair, was born in Inverness and trained at the Queen Margaret College in Edinburgh. Since leaving *Take the High Road* he has appeared at the National Theatre, Birmingham Rep, Liverpool, Guildford, Leicester, the Young Vic and the Bush Theatre, as well as in many theatres throughout Scotland. He has done much television work apart from *Take the High Road* and is an experienced radio broadcaster.

Kate Blair is the older of David Blair's daughters. She had an affair with Eddie Ramsay. Later she was discovered by Jimmy Blair camping out at the Aquasports office because she didn't want Isabel and Brian Blair to know of her presence. She knew they would tell her parents and send her home. She has since married and is living in the south.

Lucy Durham-Matthews played Kate.

Sandra Blair, David and Helen Blair's younger daughter, came to Glendarroch with her father David when he was anxious to try to sort out the supposed problems of Isabel and Brian. Glendarroch was dull to her and the only interest she found was in the ferry and Eddie Ramsay who was running it. Although the relationship with Eddie was simply a friendly one, it upset Sheila, Eddie's wife. Sandra later became involved with a bad crowd at home in the south and got into the drugs scene, from which Brian Blair was instrumental in rescuing her.

She is played by Johanna Hargreaves.

Father Brendan took over Father Joseph Houston's church in Auchtarne when Father Joseph returned to Ireland. He became very attracted to Fiona Cunningham and left the parish when it seemed that there was a danger of the attraction becoming too physical.

David Bannerman played Father Brendan.

Ken Calder was a reformed alcoholic who appeared out of the blue in Glendarroch and for a time reopened the old Glendarroch garage and carried on a motor repair business. The business failed, and when his attempt to get a new petrol station built near Glendarroch also failed, Ken became the estate mechanic, servicing the vehicles and generally looking after the machinery. Later he took on the business of peat cutting on the estate. He formed a strong bond with Lorna Seton, the estate secretary and eventually went to live with her in her cottage, though the relationship was purely platonic. When Lorna's daughter arrived for a visit and asked why they were not sharing the same bed, Ken eventually asked Lorna to marry him, warning her that he was still an alcoholic and always would be. After some hesitation she agreed and they

Left, the estate mechanic, Ken Calder (Bill Henderson) and estate secretary Lorna Seton (Joan Alcorn) in the factor's outer office at Glendarroch House. Their relationship never came to anything because Ken was an alcoholic.

Below, Jimmy and Brian Blair (Jimmy Chisholm and Kenneth Watson) in earnest discussion in the village store shortly after Brian had been released from prison.

went to get married in a registry office in Glasgow. The local people arranged a surprise reception for them when they returned, which they found highly embarrassing because once they reached Glasgow they decided their relationship was a perfectly comfortable one as it was and that marriage might spoil it, so they had abandoned the plan. When Fiona, in her youthful enthusiasm to make the estate pay and show her mother she could run it herself, demanded an unreasonable amount of effort from Ken over the peat cutting business, he took to drink and ended up in a psychiatric hospital. Bill Henderson, who played Ken Calder, was a student at the Royal Scottish Academy of Music and Drama. He won a BBC radio contract and started his career doing all kinds of radio. Later he got the part of Tod Baxter in *Garnock Way*, the drunken miner who was disowned by his family and who, in the pilot programme of *Take the High Road* actually appeared in the programme under that name. For the real thing, however, the name was changed to Ken Calder, and by that time the origins of the character had disappeared. Bill died in 1988.

Joyce Cameron, the widow of a cousin of Rev. Ian McPherson, came to Glendarroch on the death of her husband in Papua where he had been a missionary. She was a fitness fanatic and nearly killed half the population of the village by insisting that they joined her exercise classes in the village hall. Mrs Mack, fed up with Joyce issuing orders in the manse, decided to become housekeeper at Letir-Falloch and leave Joyce in charge, an arrangement with which the minister heartily agreed – until he found that Joyce provided him with even less food than Mrs Mack did. Eventually he persuaded Mrs Mack to return and Joyce left.

Georgine Anderson played Joyce Cameron.

Jock Campbell had been a very fine athlete in his youth, winning cups at different Highland Games throughout Scotland. He won the Glendarroch hill race three years running, a feat never equalled. Jock's wife and son died many years ago and Jock lived alone in a cottage in the village. He became blind and more and more helpless and friendless until Eddie Ramsay sought his advice in running the revived Glendarroch hill race. Eddie hoped to win the prize of £200 to give to Sheila Lamont to complete the education she had missed by having his child. Jock took Eddie into the cottage and Sheila came to help look after him. Eventually Jock came to terms with his disability and agreed to go into an old folks' home in Auchtarne on condition that Eddie and Sheila got his cottage.

Ian Stewart, who plays Jock Campbell, is one of the band of actors who began working when there was no real professional theatre in Scotland. Like many of his vintage he did much of his early work in radio. He was the first Divine Correction in Tyrone Guthrie's production of *The Thrie Estaits* in 1948. Married to Scots actress Sheila Latimer, Ian has a son and a daughter and four grandchildren.

George Carradine, the estate lawyer, practises in Auchtarne where his father, who is well into his nineties, still assists him in the running of the business. The Carradines have been the estate's men of business since the days of Sir Logan Peddie, serving him, Elizabeth Cunningham and Fiona.

Leon Sinden, who plays Mr Carradine, was born at Ditchling in Sussex and came to Scotland in 1951 to join the Wilson Barrett Company. He has made his home here ever since, although he has worked in the West End with Alec Guinness in *Ross*, with the Royal Shakespeare Company at Stratford and has been twice to Broadway with Leonard

Rossiter in *Semi-Detached* and with his brother Donald in *London Assurance*. He has toured extensively all over the world and done six seasons at Pitlochry as leading actor and director. Besides Mr Carradine, Leon has played many other parts on television and over the last eight years has appeared regularly in pantomime, playing Squires, Kings, Barons and so on and has collaborated with Walter Carr in writing many of them.

Paul Cassell was the owner of an advertising agency in Edinburgh, though this was unclear when he rented the Dower House at Glendarroch. His company was in trouble and his major client, Langemann International, threatened to take their account elsewhere unless Cassell found some way of getting Elizabeth Cunningham out of Glendarroch while Max Langemann put through certain deals at an estate board meeting. Cassell tried to do this, but made the mistake of genuinely falling for Elizabeth. Elizabeth, warned by Peter Cunningham of Cassell's position, faced him with it and Cassell left empty-handed.

Glyn Owen played Paul Cassell.

Tom Clifton arrived mysteriously in Glendarroch asking for Maggie Ferguson, much to Maggie's concern. He eventually confessed to Sorry Watson that his parents had recently died and he had only then discovered he was adopted and that his natural mother was a Maggie Ferguson who came from Glendarroch. After some discussion, Maggie eventually admitted that long ago she had had an illegitimate child. But it had been a daughter, not a son.

Jonathan Battersby played Tom Clifton.

Mr Cochrane, the father of Marion Cochrane and ex-husband of Lorna Seton, is an oil executive. When he heard that Lorna was giving house room to Ken Calder and Marion at the same time, he came to Glendarroch to try to persuade Marion to go with him to Saudi Arabia where he was under contract to an oil exploration company. He refused to meet Lorna and most of what he heard was received at second hand. Nothing from these sources set his mind at rest, but Jimmy Blair, who had become very friendly with Marion, indignantly told him that he should find out the situation at first hand rather than rely on gossip from people like Maggie Ferguson. Marion eventually agreed to leave Glendarroch, but refused to accompany her father to Saudi Arabia.

Martin Heller played Mr Cochrane. Although English, he has worked in Scotland for forty years. He is married and has four daughters and two sons.

Marion Cochrane, Lorna Seton's daughter, had been rejected by her mother when Lorna was going through the trauma of separation from her husband. She was a girl with great common sense and rare insight, forming a strong attachment for Jimmy Blair. Eventually she left Glendarroch to start a domestic science course in Glasgow and, returning unexpectedly one day, found that Jimmy was having an affair with Sally Shaw. She left Glendarroch quietly and finally.

Lizzie Radford played Marion.

Derek Conway rented the Dower House in Glendarroch and refused to talk about his past. People seemed to recognise him. Mrs Mack was sure she had seen his photograph in a newspaper, believed he was a mass murderer and had no hesitation in saying so. It was Sorry Watson who recognised him as Wing Commander Conway, a test pilot who, in a new type of aircraft had run into technical difficulties and, managing to avoid a heavily built-up area had crashed his aircraft into the sea just off the coast, only just managing to eject in time. Unfortunately the aircraft had bounced unexpectedly across the water and hit a school playing field, killing some children and a teacher. Although the enquiry had totally exonerated him, Conway found his life disintegrating round him, his marriage broke up and he had come to Glendarroch to hide and try to find peace. In fact he found Fiona Cunningham, recovering from the effects of her fall from a horse after she had discovered Alex Geddes, with whom she had been having a passionate affair, in the arms of his housekeeper, Chrissie McAlpine. Conway managed to restore Fiona's mental balance by persuading her to ride again, after which she persuaded him to take the controls of a light plane at Glasgow Airport and fly again.

Derek Conway was played by Ian McCulloch.

Peter Craig is a local man, one difficult to employ. Most of his time was spent working for Sneddon for a pittance because he had a wife and family to support and needed the money. Peter Craig often got into uncomfortable scrapes on Sneddon's behalf and for this reason became rather unpopular in the village.

He is played by Jay Smith who has been a Euro M.P. candidate and is a local councillor for the Scottish National Party, which leaves him little time for appearances in the programme now. Jay is married and has four children, the last two being twins.

Florence Crossan is the younger sister of Mrs Mack who occasionally comes to Glendarroch to look after Mr McPherson when Mrs Mack is away. *See* Mary Mack.

Elizabeth Cunningham was born Elizabeth Peddie, the daughter of Sir Logan Peddie and on her father's death she became the Lady Laird of Glendarroch. Married to Peter Cunningham, an Edinburgh lawyer, they had one daughter, Fiona. The problem of being a successful Edinburgh lawyer's wife as well as Lady Laird of Glendarroch proved too much and the marriage foundered. Elizabeth had many problems keeping the estate going, death duties having taken up so much money there was little left to keep it viable. Forced to sell to a German consortium headed by Max Langemann, she retained a seat on the board and thereafter her main concern was to ensure that the life of the estate was not wrecked by the demands of the new owners. She was distressed when Peter announced he was marrying again, but the marriage did not last and it looked as if a reconciliation might be possible. She spent more and more time in Edinburgh, leaving the estate in Fiona's hands. But when Fiona became pregnant and the birth of her baby was due, Elizabeth, driving to the hospital to see her new grandson, was killed in a car crash.

Elizabeth Cunningham was played by Edith MacArthur who comes from Ardrossan and has been one of Scotland's leading actresses since the days when she first appeared with the Wilson Barrett Company. Since leaving *Take the High Road* she has been seen most frequently at the Royal Lyceum Theatre in Edinburgh and at Pitlochry Festival Theatre.

Fiona Cunningham, the daughter of Peter and Elizabeth Cunningham lacked a sense of purpose in life. Perhaps because of the widely different interests of her parents, she seemed unsure whether she wanted to join the social set in Edinburgh with her father or learn the business of managing the estate with her mother. Eventually she decided on the estate. Before that she had run an Aquasports business on the loch with Jimmy Blair and had

Right, when Sir Logan Peddie died, his daughter Elizabeth Cunningham (Edith MacArthur) became Lady Laird of Glendarroch Estate. Here she is in the drawing room of Glendarroch House.

Below, something seems to have caught the eye of Peter Craig (Jay Smith) and Davie Sneddon (Derek Lord). Could the people of Glendarroch be plotting another escapade against the neighbouring estate of Letir-Falloch?

taken a secretarial course to qualify her for the job – something which was to stand her in good stead later. But she soon tired of the Aquasports business – it was Jimmy who did the interesting work, teaching water skiing, fraternising with the customers – while she sat in the office and typed letters and answered the telephone. Looking for an outlet to augment the income of the estate she tried to introduce pony trekking and surveyed the stables at the Home Farm where the estate horses were kept. There she met the new farm manager, Alex Geddes, and although the relationship started with much hostility, it developed into a tempestuous affair which only ended when she caught him in the arms of his housekeeper. Later she met Ruari Galbraith, financial adviser to Sorry Watson and, mutually attracted, they spent a weekend together in Glasgow. She became pregnant and Ruari wanted to marry her. She refused and when her son, David, was born, she rejected the baby. She held him responsible for the death of her mother, killed in a car crash on her way to see him the day he was born. Saddled with enormous death duties, Fiona was forced to sell the estate to the Ross-Giffords. She bought for herself the nearby country house, Ardnacraig, which she converted into a hotel. Ruari continued to ask her to marry him and she continued to refuse. Then asked if he might take David for a short spell to meet his parents. Fiona agreed and Ruari took David away. She was not sure whether she would ever see him again . . .

Caroline Ashley, who plays Fiona Cunningham, was born in Lanark and was educated at Coatbridge High School and the Queen Margaret College in Edinburgh. The part of Fiona was virtually her first professional engagement. Since then she has managed to fit in several other things between series. Her hobbies include fencing, horse riding and lying about doing nothing, though she has little time for any of them these days, especially the last.

Peter Cunningham, Fiona's father, is a successful Edinburgh lawyer. When Elizabeth's concern for Glendarroch proved more important to her than their marriage, there was a divorce and he returned to his practice in Edinburgh. Peter remarried, but it didn't last and he and Elizabeth were in the process of re-establishing their relationship when she was killed in a car crash. Unable to face this, Peter took to drink, hating his grandson whom he blamed for the death of Elizabeth, and it was only Fiona's care and help which saved him.

Peter Cunningham is played by Donald Douglas.

Douglas Dunbar applied for the job of factor at Glendarroch after the departure of Alan McIntyre to Brazil. The son of a Scots father and an English mother, he was educated at an English boarding school. He ran the estate for Elizabeth for a few years until he left to return to his old job as factor on an estate in the north and to marry the owner's daughter.

Douglas Dunbar was played by Clive Graham.

Susan Duncan and her husband Bill had given Jimmy Blair houseroom when he came to Glasgow from Glendarroch. Her name first came to Isabel's attention when an *In Memoriam* notice for Jimmy appeared in a newspaper on the first anniversary of his death, signed simply with the letter S. It was Sheila Ramsay who traced the person who had inserted the notice and met Susan in a park in Glasgow. Later she and Isabel met. Susan had her baby, Jamie, with her. Isabel believed Jamie must be Jimmy's son, but

Susan said no. Only later did Susan and Bill discover that Jamie must indeed be Jimmy's. Trying for a second baby and being consistently unsuccessful, medical tests proved that Bill could not father a child. Bill became physically hostile to Susan and Jamie, and she left him to go to Glendarroch to rejoin Isabel.

Susan is played by Jacqueline Gilbrook who trained at the Aberdeen College of Education and the Welsh College of Music and Drama, although she herself comes from Glasgow. Jacqueline is married and has recently become the proud mother of a daughter.

Maggie Ferguson's father had been Sir Logan Peddie's batman during the First World War and Maggie ran the bus service between Glendarroch and Auchtarne. She was a difficult woman to get on with, an inveterate and malicious gossip who never had a good word to say for anyone. She had been courted in her youth by Sorry Watson and eventually, after he had made his fortune, she agreed to marry him and they went to live in Shetland. She has returned occasionally to upset Isabel and the rest of the village.

Maggie Ferguson is played by Irene Sunters who is well known in all fields of entertainment in Scotland, having appeared in almost every major theatre. She has also a long list of television credits.

Sir William Fleming is an uncle of Elizabeth Cunningham's, Fiona's great uncle, an old-fashioned martinet with very definite ideas of a woman's place in the scheme of things – preferably in the kitchen or the nursery.

Sir William is played by Brown Derby.

Maisie Forbes is a niece of Jean McTaggart's. She lives in Auchtarne and came to look after her aunt when she was ill. The talent of reading teacups runs in the family. Mrs McTaggart has it and so has Maisie.

Janet Michael plays Maisie.

Kirsty Forsyth was Glendarroch's first vet. Her father was the vet in Auchtarne and after graduating Kirsty took on the Glendarroch district for him. Kirsty left Glendarroch for a town practice in Edinburgh.

Kirsty was played by Anna Davidson.

Robert Forsyth, Kirsty's father, extended his area of activity when his daughter Kirsty went to join a veterinary practice in Edinburgh. Shortly afterwards, Forsyth went into semi-retirement, keeping the Glendarroch branch of his practice and buying a cottage in the village. He eventually retired completely and the practice was taken over by Colin Begg.

Ian Wallace, who played Robert Forsyth, is perhaps best known these days for his appearances in *My Music* on radio and television. Born in London of Scottish parents, Ian was educated at Charterhouse and Trinity Hall Cambridge, and thereafter pursued a distinguished singing career in opera interspersed with lighter musical ventures in the realms of Gilbert and Sullivan as well as Flanders and Swann. He has written two volumes of autobiography and was awarded the OBE in 1983. He lives in London with his wife, Pat. They have a daughter and a son.

Jennifer 'Fraser' was a cousin of Sheila Lamont's who came to stay with Eddie and Sheila with her baby, Karen. She claimed she had married an old boy friend from Auchtarne, Tom Fraser, who was in prison. But there was something odd about Jennifer, and when Tom Fraser suddenly showed up she didn't even recognise him. It turned out she was not married, that she had had an illegitimate baby

Right, Fiona Cunningham (Caroline Ashley) with one of the horses which she keeps stabled at the Home Farm.

Below, Maggie Ferguson (Irene Sunters) engaged in yet another argument with Sorry Watson (Ron Paterson). Isabel Blair (Eileen McCallum) has heard it all before.

which had died, whereupon she had stolen a baby and escaped to Glendarroch with her, passing her off as her own. When this was discovered she disappeared from Eddie and Sheila's cottage with the baby. She stole the ferry and headed out for an island in the loch. She was pursued by Eddie and the police. Eddie, who doted on Karen, managed to rescue the baby, but Jennifer jumped from a cliff into the water and was drowned.

Jennifer was played by Joyce Deans.

Mrs Galbraith, Ruari Galbraith's mother is a formidable woman. It takes a very strong personality to stand up to her, as her husband, her son and Fiona Cunningham have found. She lives in Glasgow, dotes on Ruari and has no time for Fiona Cunningham whatsoever. It was through her influence that Ruari took his son from Fiona and left him in the care of his mother.

Mrs Galbraith is played by Diana Olsson.

Ruari Galbraith is a financial expert who comes from Glasgow. He has for some years been Sorry Watson's financial adviser, and it was Sorry who introduced Ruari to Glendarroch. He met and fell in love with Fiona Cunningham, but their backgrounds were too different for the relationship to become in any way permanent, though eventually, after Fiona had had his child, he was willing to give up his financial career to marry her and live in Glendarroch. Knowing him better than he knew himself, Fiona refused him, believing he could never settle to a life in the country.

Ruari Galbraith is played by Charles Jamieson.

Alex Geddes, the dour manager of the Glendarroch Home Farm, attracted Fiona

Cunningham into an affair she believed to be serious but to him was no more than a passing fancy. He was a loner who had never been accepted by the people of Glendarroch. After Fiona discovered him having an affair with his housekeeper, Chrissie McAlpine, she took a horse from the Home Farm stables and rode off. She was thrown while trying to take a fence. After her physical recovery, but still mentally unbalanced, Geddes tried to help her without success. He left the area to farm in the Borders.

James Cosmo played Alex Geddes.

Willie Gillespie was found by Dougal Lachlan half dead in a ditch from starvation and exposure. He had run away from home in Glasgow and was seeking work. Taken on by Inverdarroch, he helped on the farm. He met and became besotted with Carol Mackay. Finding in Inverdarroch's desk drawer an old notebook containing some handwritten poetry he thought was by Inverdarroch, he attempted to write poetry for Carol. He failed miserably. He showed some of Inverdarroch's poems to Brian Blair who got him to copy them out. Lily Taylor read them and arranged to publish them for Inverdarroch. But the poems were not written by Inverdarroch but by his grandfather many years before. Willie, having no success with Carol decided that country life was not for him and returned to Glasgow.

Willie Gillespie was played first by Joe Mullaney and then by Ewen Emery.

Kay Grant was Glendarroch's first district nurse. She was brought to the district by Alan McIntyre, the estate factor, whom she had nursed in a Glasgow hospital when he had a broken leg. For a long time it looked as if Kay and Alan might get married, but it never came to anything. She spent much of her time trying to improve the conditions of the outlying

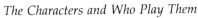

Left, Ruari Galbraith (Charles Jamieson) and Fiona Cunningham (Caroline Ashley) just after the birth of their son, David. The scene was filmed in a Glasgow Maternity Unit and the baby was borrowed for the occasion – with Mother's permission!

Right, Fiona Cunningham (Caroline Ashley) and Alex Geddes (James Cosmo) the manager of the Home Farm, look happy and carefree, but their torrid affair, which became the scandal of the village, nearly ended in Fiona's death.

The estate's first factor and Glendarroch's first district nurse. Alan McIntyre (Martin Cochrane) and Kay Grant (Vivien Heilbron) in the original factor's office set at the Big House.

Right, the gentle tints of autumn on Loch Darroch, and the heather is in bloom.

Right, the changing face of Blair's Store, which has always been the focal point of Glendarroch life and gossip. The gossip here is between Sheila Ramsay (Lesley Fitz-Simons) and Brian and Isabel Blair (Kenneth Watson and Eileen McCallum) in the shop which Brian rebuilt shortly after his release from prison.

Above, the original Blair's Store, which many viewers regarded with affectionate nostalgia, before Brian's conversion. David Blair (Derek Anders) tries to convince Isabel that Brian's absence in prison is unjustified.

Right, the only episode of *Take the High Road* not screened nationally: the 'special' shown in Scotland on Hogmanay 1987. Fiona Cunningham, Carol Mackay (Teri Lally) and Sheila Ramsay receive presents from a thinly disguised Alec Monteath.

Left, the vet Robert Forsyth (Ian Wallace) and Mrs Mack's sister Florence Crossan (Gwyneth Guthrie), seem set for an autumnal romance. The photograph was taken on the pier at Luss. Confusingly, the Luss pier is used as the pier at Auchtarne. The Glendarroch pier is a landing stage a mile or so south of Luss

Below, the Lady Laird, Elizabeth Cunningham (Edith MacArthur) and her daughter Fiona (Caroline Ashley) in the garden of Glendarroch House.

Left, Eddie Ramsay (Robin Cameron) and Sheila Lamont (Lesley Fitz-Simons) had a chequered romance before they eventually married on a beautiful summer's day in Glendarroch Church.

crofters and farmers on the estate, especially after the death of Dougal Lachlan's wife Amy in childbirth, insisting they should be provided with telephones and better roads. Nurse Grant eventually left Glendarroch to take up a position as assistant matron in a Glasgow hospital.

Vivien Heilbron played Nurse Grant.

Captain Robert Groves was a cousin of Elizabeth Cunningham's. In their youth he had always been her hero, the boy who went further, lived more dangerously than anyone else she knew. But there was a fatal flaw in his character. He was in fact a weakling who had been drummed out of his regiment and had lived on his wits for many years. He ran up an enormous bill at Blair's Store, much to Brian Blair's anger and Isabel's embarrassment, and to repay it, he stole and pawned a diamond brooch of Elizabeth's. Discovered, Elizabeth covered up for him with the police. Groves, exposed as a charlatan and deeply ashamed, walked out. Having many times before attempted to climb Ben Darroch, this time he achieved his objective and died on the top, leaving Elizabeth the pawn ticket for her brooch and a small annuity. He asked to be buried in Glendarroch, the only place where he had ever been remotely happy.

Captain Groves was played by one of Scotland's foremost comedians and character actors, Jimmy Logan.

Graeme B. Hogg was a young financial expert brought in by Klaus Meier to put the Glendarroch Estate on a sound financial footing. He trod on many toes before he completed his report and recommendations and finally left the district with most of them unfulfilled.

Jim Byars played Graeme B. Hogg.

Father Joseph Houston was the priest in charge of Auchtarne's Catholic church. A close friend of the Rev. Ian McPherson, they used to play cribbage regularly, much to the annoyance of Mrs Mack who considered a Catholic priest was only one step short of the devil himself. She became even more alarmed when she overheard the two men of God discussing with apparent admiration the attributes of Lucifer. Believing they were in league with the devil, she summoned Mr Parker, the austere minister of St Ninian's in Auchtarne to denounce them. The discussion had been perfectly innocent – the two men had merely been wondering if horses with Biblical names stood a better chance of winning races than those without.

Father Houston was played by Pat Daly, the distinguished Irish actor whose death in 1987 deprived *Take the High Road* of a very valuable character.

Jim Hunter came to cut wood on the Glendarroch estate. He lodged with the Blairs, and Isabel, recovering from the death of Jimmy, began to mother him. Jim Hunter took advantage of this to borrow money from her, exerting an evil charm over her. Brian was aware of this influence but was powerless to prevent it without exposing Isabel to considerable disappointment and grief. When Carol Mackay formed an attachment for Jim and later thought, mistakenly, that she was pregnant, Jim attempted to murder her to keep her quiet. Brian told Jim to clear out or he would expose him if necessary to the police and he left the district, much to Isabel's distress. Later he returned to cut wood on Letir-Falloch where he fell foul of the two other woodcutters, the brothers Tam and Scott Logan, and also of Sneddon, besides meeting again Brian who threatened him with violence if he ever came near Isabel. Jim

Left, the iron grip of winter on the loch and Ben Darroch's white head dominates the scene again.

Top left, Jim Hunter (Alan Cumming) and Carol Mackay (Teri Lally). Top right, Captain Groves (Jimmy Logan) dies on the top of Ben Darroch. Above, the priest (Pat Daly) and the minister (John Young) at the racecourse.

Hunter died in a fire at the Glendarroch woodshed and a huge police investigation began as foul play was suspected. Considering Hunter's reputation, there were plenty of murder suspects. It was eventually established that he had been about to set fire to the woodshed to get even with Brian Blair who was operating the sawmill for the Glendarroch estate at the time, and had been discovered by Tam Logan. Hunter was struck by a falling beam as the woodshed burnt.

Alan Cumming played Jim Hunter.

Inverdarroch: *See* Tom Kerr.

Fergus Jamieson, the Glendarroch postman, is the source of all gossip and information in the village, and probably holds the tea-drinking record for the entire area.

He is played by Frank Wylie.

Kalsang is the Tibetan companion of Lady William Ross-Gifford and is the only person that indomitable lady is scared of.

She is played by Cedar Chozam.

Frances Kay, a leading journalist on a woman's magazine in London, came to Glendarroch to research an article on Lily Taylor whose first book was about to be serialised. She returned to London after completing her research, but not before she had established a mild sort of relationship with Brian Blair who was having domestic problems with Isabel.

Frances Kay was played by Rose McBain.

Jean Kennedy was the daughter of Isabel Blair's bridesmaid. She came to stay with the Blairs when her parents went to a relative's funeral in Canada. She was an unpleasant, selfish girl, totally ungrateful for being put up

by the Blairs, bored with the life in Glendarroch and when Drew Sneddon, Davie Sneddon's son, arrived, she quickly entered into an affair with him. Together they made the life of Carol Mackay a misery. Carol had recently acquired a dog which Drew and Jean released at nights, encouraging it to worry sheep. The dog was eventually caught and Carol tearfully denied any knowledge of its worrying sheep. Inverdarroch, concerned at Carol's distress, undertook to teach the dog a lesson by releasing it in a pen alone with a ram, which punished the dog severely. Drew and Jean also upset Constable McPhee by planting poached pheasants in his police car and getting him into trouble with Sergeant Murray. At one point, McPhee, pursuing the two of them towards the lochside, forced Drew Sneddon into the water where he disappeared in spite of McPhee's attempts to rescue him. Jean found Drew hiding in the old Aquasports office and kept him hidden there, stealing food for him from the Blairs, while she blamed McPhee for letting him drown. Eventually Brian discovered Drew and Jean was sent back in disgrace to her parents.

Jean was played by Fiona Chalmers.

Tom Kerr is an unfamiliar name to most people in Glendarroch as he is always known by the name of his farm, Inverdarroch. His family have been tenants there for many years. A big, shy, gentle man, Inverdarroch is more at home with his beasts than with people. For a time it looked as though he might have married Lily Taylor, the widow of Bob Taylor's brother Matthew. But he could never pluck up enough courage to ask her. When Fiona had to sell Inverdarroch to Harry Shaw of Letir-Falloch, Sneddon as the factor tried hard to force Inverdarroch out. But he refused to go. Then Sneddon discovered that although Inverdarroch had been paying the rent for the farm regularly, the lease had actually run out three years before and had never been renewed. He told Inverdarroch he wanted him out the next week. But Mr Carradine, the lawyer, told Inverdarroch that if the rent had been regularly paid it was assumed that the lease was still valid and he could not be dispossessed. Lily, hearing of these troubles, bought the farm from Harry Shaw to give Inverdarroch security of tenure, hoping too this would bring him to the point of proposing. But it had the opposite effect. It put Lily in the relationship of employer and servant, and Inverdarroch could not marry her under those conditions. Eventually he married Claire Millar, the district nurse, but the marriage was never a success. He wanted a wife who would help him on the farm, she wanted to continue her career. He wanted children, she didn't. In the end, discovering that Claire was having an affair with Davie Sneddon, Inverdarroch left the farm with his shotgun, intent on shooting Sneddon.

John Stahl, who plays Invardarroch, was born in Sauchie in Clackmannanshire and was educated at Alloa Academy. He trained at the Royal Scottish Academy of Music and Drama at the same time as those other celebrated *Take the High Road* characters, Hamish and Mairi McNeil, Alice Taylor and Peter Craig. He has worked in the theatre all over Scotland and professes to be an armchair sportsman, though in fact he plays a mean game of cricket. He says his ambition is to score the winning goal for Scotland in the 1998 World Cup having captained Scotland's rugby team to that year's Grand Slam. He and his wife Doreen live in Glasgow.

Donald Lachlan, the son of Dougal and Amy Lachlan has been played by four different boys of different ages through the ten-year run of the programme. Donald as a baby was played by Alan Dunbar, as he grew older by Stuart Herd, then by Kevin Shearer until the programme moved to Glasgow, whereupon Steven Brown took over the part and has played him ever since. Steven appeared in several Scottish Television Dramarama plays before landing the part of Donald, and he has also appeared in a recent series of *Taggart*. He started secondary school this year and hopes to be able to go to the Royal Scottish Academy of Music and Drama when the time comes and make acting his full time career.

Dougal Lachlan is the canny crofter of Ardvain and people take him for a fool at their peril. Dougal's wife, Amy, died giving birth to their son, Donald, and for a time Dougal couldn't forgive his son for depriving him of the woman he loved. There was always the big problem of who was going to look after Donald. Dougal's mother, Grace, was getting old and couldn't be expected to look after Dougal and his baby son as well. So Dougal had to let Donald go to his sister-in-law, Alice, after she had married the water bailiff, Bob Taylor. There was a time when the possibility of Dougal remarrying was one of the talking points of Glendarroch. First it was Morag Stewart with whom he had had a long love-hate relationship. Dougal's croft and Morag's croft marched together and the combination of the two would have been an advantage. But the relationship never came to anything in spite of the encouragement of Morag's father, Jamie Stewart, who even offered to let Dougal have his old tractor very cheap if he took Morag off his hands. This was tempting to Dougal, but not tempting enough. Then Dougal met Gladys Aitken and after some time they got married and Dougal and Gladys, together with Donald and Gladys's daughter, Emma, formed a nuclear family in the croft.

Right, it looks as though postman Fergus Jamieson (Frank Wylie) has just learnt another piece of gossip in Blair's Store which he can pass on in return for a cup of tea.

Below, Steven Brown has played Donald Lachlan for three years now. Steven rehearses and records scenes in the studio after school hours, and now does most of his filming on Saturdays.

Alec Monteath, who plays Dougal, is married to Linna Skelton and they have two sons, David who is an actor and Alasdair who is an analyst/programmer. Educated at McLaren High School in Callander, Glasgow University and the Royal Scottish Academy of Music and Drama, Alec has appeared over many years in every major theatre in Scotland, playing a wide variety of roles from high tragedy to dame in pantomime. For five years he was an announcer/newsreader with Scottish Television, followed by seven years with the presentation department of BBC Scotland. He joined *Take the High Road* for its first episode and has been with the programme ever since. Alec's interests are reading, Scottish heraldry and Scottish history – he is a Fellow of the Society of Antiquaries Scotland – boating, shooting and fishing.

Grace Lachlan, the mother of Dougal, was married to Donald Lachlan whose family crofted at Ardvain. In fact the Lachlans recently celebrated their century on the same land. Grace has kept house for Dougal for almost all his life, but when he married Gladys Aitken Grace suddenly found herself out of place in the croft. For a time she moved from one house to another, but could not settle. Eventually she took it into her head to go to live with her sister Maeve near Glasgow. She had not been in touch with Maeve for several years, and when she reached the house she found that Maeve had been taken into a home and had died there. Lost and alone, Grace was found by Dougal wandering in Queen Street station in Glasgow and brought back to the croft where she was installed again in her own and rightful place.

Marjorie Thomson who plays Grace Lachlan was born in Glasgow. She has two daughters, Anne and Lesley, and four grandchildren. She appeared with Glasgow Unity Theatre and, with Stanley Baxter and Jimmy Logan, was in the inaugural programme from Scottish Television. One of her treasured memories is being in the Royal Variety Performance at the Alhambra Theatre in Glasgow in July 1958. Her list of television credits is extremely long and includes *Dr Finlay's Casebook*, *Sutherland's Law* and on radio, *The McFlannels*. She also had a leading part in Scottish Television's first soap opera, *High Living*. Marjorie lists her hobbies as reading, doing crosswords and watching quiz shows on television and thinking she could do better – sometimes.

Alison Lambert was the daughter of the sales director of Marinewear, a sports clothing and equipment firm. She herself ran an aquasports centre on Loch Earn and was sent by her father to assess the potential of the Glendarroch Aquasports business. Unfortunately she seemed more interested in the potential of Jimmy Blair.

Alison was played by Carol Anne Crawford.

Dan Lamont, Sheila Lamont's father, was a local Glendarroch man who violently disapproved of her association with Eddie Ramsay. He died of a heart attack about six years ago.

He was played by Ray Jeffries.

Irene Lamont, Dan Lamont's wife and Sheila's mother remarried some time after Dan's death. Irene wanted to get married in Glendarroch church, but Sam Scanlon, her husband to be, said no. It was to be a registry office in Glasgow. This upset Irene considerably, but she went through with the ceremony under protest. After it was over Sam whipped her off to the Glasgow Garden Centre where Mr McPherson, the Glendarroch minister was waiting to marry them again in the Garden Festival church, after which Sam had arranged

Left, Sheila Lamont (Lesley Fitz-Simons) has been in the programme for eight years now and much has happened to her in that time, including an illegitimate child and a broken marriage.

Below, one of *Take the High Road*'s best loved characters is Grace Lachlan (Marjorie Thomson). Few people have seen Marjorie darning socks. She is usually to be found in the green room playing cards with some of her colleagues!

a reception on the paddle steamer *Waverley*. Irene was astonished and delighted and Sam was forgiven. They now live in Glasgow.

Trudy Bryce plays Irene Lamont.

Sheila Lamont/Ramsay, the daughter of Dan and Irene Lamont, went to the Auchtarne High School a year ahead of Carol Mackay. She had a brilliant scholastic career and her parents were proudly looking forward to her going to university. But the year she finished school she became pregnant to Eddie Ramsay, the ne'er-do-well son of Fraser Ramsay. Eddie had a reputation for theft and disorder in the village. This infuriated her father and distressed her mother, so much so that after endless recriminations and just before the baby was due, Sheila went off to Glasgow, had the baby and then had it adopted without even seeing it or knowing whether it was a boy or a girl. When she returned to Glendarroch without the baby Eddie was very upset. He wanted Sheila to marry him, but it was only after he had failed to win the Glandarroch hill race and gain the £200 prize he had hoped to give her as some compensation for her loss of education, that she really fell for him and they were married. The marriage, however, was never very successful. Eddie could not forget the child he had hoped for and Sheila had arbitrarily given away. Sheila wanted to live a better and more fulfilling life than was available to her in Glendarroch. Eventually Eddie left to join the army. When Robert Forsyth, the vet, retired, he told Sheila that he was also giving up his job of providing *The Auchtarne Herald* with items of local news and wondered if Sheila would like to take over from him. She accepted with alacrity, and when the paper changed hands and was bought by Mark Ritchie she eventually got a full-time job as caption writer-cum-cub-reporter-cum-general coffee maker.

Lesley Fitz-Simons, who plays Sheila, was born in Glasgow and is married to Peter McIntyre, the sales director of a building company. Lesley has worked extensively in television, appearing in such programmes as *Square Mile of Murder*, *House on the Hill* and *The Prime of Miss Jean Brodie*, before the part of Sheila Lamont came up. She has also done pantomime. Her hobbies, for which she says she has little time between learning lines and cleaning the house, are long walks and drives in the country, reading and eating out.

Max Langemann, the head of the great German business complex Langemann International, bought the Glendarroch estate from Elizabeth Cunningham with the intention of turning it into a hunting, shooting and fishing paradise for his rich business associates. Before he could carry out this plan, however, the economic situation began to affect his empire. He decided to retire to an island he owned in the Aegean and sold out to Klaus Meier.

Frederick Jaeger played Max Langemann.

Sarah Lindsey, a rich friend of Lady Margaret Ross-Gifford's, was partly instrumental in Lady Margaret's leaving Glendarroch. She had a very soft spot for Sir John who did not reciprocate.

Sarah Lindsey is played by Juliet Cadzow.

Scott Logan came to Glendarroch with his elder brother when Davie Sneddon advertised for men to open up the Letir-Falloch sawmill. He and Carol MacKay formed a relationship which his brother Tam disapproved of. After Tam was arrested for the murder of Jim Hunter, Scott, to whom Tam was a hero, told Carol that he could not give evidence against him at his trial and decided to disappear with her help. But before he could carry out the plan, Tam decided to plead guilty to the lesser charge of manslaughter, and Scott would not be required to testify. The news of this reached him just as he and Carol were about to leave Glendarroch for London. He stayed on in Glendarroch and for a time took over the running of the ferry.

He is played by Micky McPherson.

Tam Logan took on the responsibility of parenthood for his younger brother when their father died at an early age. He was perhaps a little over-protective of him, not giving him a chance to live his own life.

He was played by John Murtagh.

Chrissie McAlpine was the housekeeper at the Home Farm during Alex Geddes's tenure. It was his affair with her which was discovered by Fiona Cunningham and caused her mental breakdown.

Beth Robens played Chrissie McAlpine.

Jockie MacDonald is a general handyman who used to have his own business in Auchtarne. The business failed recently and he had to rely on picking up odd jobs wherever he could. He sometimes helps out at Glendarroch House, which is not popular with Archie Menzies, as Jockie works at three times Archie's speed and with twice his competence.

Jackie Farrell, who plays Jockie MacDonald, and his wife Patsy live in Clydebank. They have three sons. Jackie was born in Paisley and started his life in the profession as a singer, dancer and comedy feed in variety. He frequently plays dame in pantomime and has appeared in many television productions. His hobbies are golf, learning to play the piano and D.I.Y.

Alice McEwan/Taylor is the sister of Amy Lachlan, Dougal Lachlan's first wife who died giving birth to Donald. She came to Ardvain

to help to look after Donald, and there met and fell in love with Bob Taylor, the water bailiff. They were married in Glendarroch Church, but only after Alice had persuaded Bob to allow Donald to come and live with them, thus relieving the pressure on Grace and Dougal at the croft. Bob reluctantly agreed to this. Later, Alice became pregnant but lost the baby due to an ectopic pregnancy. She had to undergo a complete hysterectomy so there could never be any more children. This upset Alice's mental balance and she began to blame Bob for what had happened to her. Her attitude was made worse by Dougal refusing to allow her to go on looking after Donald in her present unstable mental condition and insisting on taking him back to the croft. Eventually, Isabel Blair told Alice about her own hysterectomy and her rejection of Brian which had driven him to form the relationship with the waitress and subsequently kill her. Alice realised how long-suffering Bob had been and their relationship was restored. Later, Alice, discovering a talent for cookery, got a job as cook at the Ardnacraig Hotel.

Alice was played first by Muriel Romanes who was born in Cambridge and trained at the Royal Scottish Academy of Music and Drama and has worked extensively, both before playing Alice and after, in theatres all over Scotland. After Muriel left the company to pursue her theatrical career, the part was taken over by Barbara Rafferty who also trained at the R.S.A.M.D. and has worked all over Scotland as well as appearing in many television programmes and films, including *Tutti Frutti* and *The Wicker Man*.

Effie McInnes, Glendarroch's classic spinster, spends her life trying to find herself a man and never succeeds. Effie first came to work for the Big House when Derek Conway took the Dower House and she was engaged as general housekeeper there. Afterwards she moved to the Big House itself as housekeeper. When Fiona Cunningham sold the estate and bought the Ardnacraig Hotel, Effie managed to hold down the job at the Big House and also did a little moonlighting at the Ardnacraig for Fiona, until she was caught by Lady Margaret and summarily dismissed from Big House service. After this she worked full time at the Ardnacraig.

Mary Riggans, who plays Effie McInnes was born in Glasgow, now lives in Edinburgh and has a daughter, Samantha who is a B.Sc. She herself obtained what she describes as a very ordinary M.A. degree from Glasgow University, but having started working in Children's Hour on radio as a schoolgirl, she never really got a chance to use it. Her radio career spans a great variety of work from *Saturday Night Theatre* to Schools programmes and *Morning Story*, while in television she first appeared at the age of sixteen in *A Nest of Singing Birds* by Robert Kemp. Since then there have been many other appearances in such programmes as *Dr Finlay's Casebook*, *Sunset Song* and *Maggie*. If anyone in the cast needs a pair of socks Mary will knit them with little provocation. Her other hobbies are crosswords, driving and cycling and, she says, making sure she never gets fat again.

Alan McIntyre was the first factor of Glendarroch. An efficient man with a wide understanding of the job, Alan had managed an estate in Brazil for his father-in-law. His marriage had broken up, the reason for his return to Scotland, but he later decided to go back to Brazil and to his wife, Paula.

Alan McIntyre was played by Martin Cochrane.

Mary Mack, the widow of Hector Mack, is the Glendarroch gossip and scandalmonger.

The middle sister of three, Mary came from Glasgow to be the minister's housekeeper at the manse when her older sister, Lizzie Fraser, gave up the job. She is fiercely protective of Mr McPherson, feeding him only what she considers to be nourishing foods and ever mindful of both his moral and physical welfare, except when it affects her own. When Mr McPherson's retirement was first suggested, Mrs Mack was all in favour of the idea, until she realised that Mr Parker, who would have succeeded him in the joint charge of Glendarroch and St Ninian's in Auchtarne, would not be using the Glendarroch manse and would not require the services of a housekeeper. When Mr McPherson was given notice to quit the manse, Mrs Mack barricaded herself in and refused to come out, an incident which, thanks to Sheila Ramsay, hit the front pages of the national press. Later, when the manse was restored to Mr McPherson and herself, she threw the minister out of his study and opened a tearoom there which she operated with furious efficiency.

Anyone less like the ferocious Mrs Mack than Gwyneth Guthrie it would be hard to imagine. Born in Ayr, Gwyneth was educated at Ayr Academy, Ayr Grammar School and St Brides, Helensburgh before going to the Royal Scottish Academy of Music and Drama and gaining the Silver Medal in her year. She is married to John Borland and they live in a farmhouse near Kilmarnock and have three daughters, Karen, Debbie and Olwen, and one grand-daughter, Kirstie. She has worked extensively in the theatre and television, and began her career in radio at the age of twelve. She enjoys listening to music and flower arranging, though there isn't much time for that these days. Besides the indomitable Mrs Mack, Gwyneth also plays her sister, Florence, which is much more like type-casting.

Right, Muriel Romanes who played Alice Taylor for the first eight years of the programme before deciding to move back to a career in the theatre where she has achieved some stunning successes.

Below, filming for an episode at the Royal Highland Show at Ingliston near Edinburgh, Heather McNeil (Bridget McCann) looks as if she's testing a new tractor for her cousin Hamish NcNeil (William Armour) and Dougal Lachlan (Alec Monteath).

Carol MacKay was a year or two behind Sheila Lamont at the Auchtarne High School and has always been one of Glendarroch's problem youngsters. She has drifted around the village since leaving school doing odd jobs here and there. She worked for Fiona Cunningham at the Ardnacraig Hotel as a waitress until she was supplanted by Emma Aitken, then Isabel Blair took pity on her and offered her a job in the store. This went well until Isabel, going south to visit her sister-in-law Helen, left Carol in charge. A wild party took place in the store one night, the post office safe was broken into and the money stolen. This last turned out to be a trick on Emma Aitken's part – she and Carol have never got on – but Isabel, hearing what had happened from Mrs Mack when she returned, gave Carol notice. Carol then thought up the idea of running a tearoom with Effie McInnes in the village hall, but it was vetoed by Mrs Mack who, as caretaker of the hall, would not allow them to use it. Mrs Mack took over the idea herself and opened a tearoom in the manse, offering Carol a job as waitress. She has been in trouble with men, too. First Jim Hunter, who tried to murder her when she told him she thought she was pregnant. In fact she was not, which may have saved her life. Then she formed a relationship with Scott Logan, but like everything Carol touches, it didn't last.

Teri Lally plays Carol Mackay.

Hamish McNeil is married to Mairi McNeil and they have three children – Lynne the oldest, Catriona and Sandy, very much younger. He runs a croft fairly close to the Lachlans' and is constantly crossing swords with Dougal.

William Armour plays Hamish McNeil.

Heather McNeil is a niece of Hamish's. She came to Glendarroch at Hamish's instigation when he and others were trying to find a wife for Dougal – at the same time as they were trying to find a husband for Morag Stewart.

Bridget McCann played Heather McNeil.

Lynne McNeil is Hamish and Mairi McNeil's older daughter. A very clever girl, her father had ideas of her going to university, but Lynne simply wanted to follow in her father's footsteps and be a crofter. Besides, in spite of grants, it was too expensive to send her to any kind of college. When Lady Margaret Ross-Gifford deserted Sir John and he was left lonely and disillusioned, a chance meeting with Lynne at the riverside was the start of a friendship that restored his mental equilibrium. Her simple directness and understanding of the countryside gave him comfort. Her parents were aghast at this relationship, remembering the stories of the old laird, Sir Logan Peddie, and his philandering ways. But Sir John was not Sir Logan and in gratitude for her friendship he offered to pay Lynne's fees to agricultural college, promising her a job at the Home Farm when she had graduated. But Lynne did not find the college to her liking – there was too much theory and not enough practice. She returned to Glendarroch surreptitiously and camped out in the Home Farm not daring to tell either her parents or Sir John that she had given up college. She was found out and Sir John, while angry at her deception, agreed to allow her to work at the Home Farm under Michael Ross.

Gillian McNeill, who plays Lynne McNeil, is descended from the sheepstealing McNeils of Barra. Her great grandfather introduced the family to the southern part of Scotland when he walked from Barra with his cow and his dog and ended up in Broughty Ferry. And that's where the family stayed, except that Gillian was born a couple of miles down the road in Monifeith. By then the family had added another 'l' to the name she and the character share. She was educated at Monifeith High School and the Royal Scottish Academy of Music and Drama. Appearing in *Take the High Road* was her first job after leaving college, though since then she has appeared in pantomime and worked for the BBC between times.

Mairi McNeil, the wife of Hamish McNeil has a fairly stormy relationship with her husband. She is a strong-minded woman who finds it difficult to put up with Hamish's almost total reliance on her. She is a great friend and confidante of Isabel Blair's.

Anne Myatt, who plays Mairi, is married to Bob Sendall and they have a daughter, Shuna. Anne was born in Glasgow and educated at Eastwood Secondary School and the Royal Scottish Academy of Music and Drama. She has a long string of television appearances to her credit and many stage performances, mostly at the Citizen's in Glasgow or the Lyceum in Edinburgh. She lists her hobbies as sewing, gardening, D.I.Y. and being a builder's labourer. This last is explained by the fact that her mother's family were crofters in the Highlands and her cousin still owns the house. Nearby Anne and her husband have a ruin of a house and are in the process of rebuilding it.

Graham McPhee, commonly known as Big Ears, was a police constable in Auchtarne. When the search was on for Scott Logan to appear in court to give evidence against his brother, Sheila Ramsay hid Scott and Carol in her cottage when McPhee called. Finding out later, McPhee never forgave Sheila, especially as she had also spurned his clumsy amorous advances. He made anonymous telephone calls to her at all hours of the day and night until Mark Ritchie finally worked out that he was the culprit. Ritchie confronted McPhee

and demanded he ask for a transfer to another district or Sergeant Murray would hear the whole story. McPhee got his transfer.

P.C. McPhee was played by Stewart Bishop and, contrary to his nickname, he does not have particularly big ears. The name arose when he was first dressed for the part and the only policeman's cap available in the wardrobe was slightly too big for him. It lodged on top of his ears, pushing them out.

Rev. Ian McPherson has been the minister at Glendarroch for most of his working life. A widower with no family he is held in great affection by the entire village. This was proved when he decided that it was time for him to retire. The village at first accepted this news with great regret, but when they heard the Presbytery was suggesting a linkage between Glendarroch and St Ninian's in Auchtarne and the austere Mr Parker of St Ninian's came to preach in Glendarroch one Sunday, the entire congregation rebelled after his hellfire and damnation sermon. The same day Mr McPherson preached in St Ninian's and was very warmly received by a congregation unused to hearing such a gentle, humane address. There was even a move to push Mr Parker out of St Ninian's and get Mr McPherson to undertake both charges. But this was beyond his capabilities and although he was persuaded to stay on a little longer, he eventually retired and his place was taken, not by Mr Parker, but by his assistant, Michael Ross.

Mr McPherson is played by John Young who began his stage career before the war. He has worked extensively in every theatre in Scotland and on television and radio where his voice is in great demand. He and his wife, Freddie, a theatrical agent in Glasgow, are the parents of Paul Young who plays John's arch-rival, the Rev. Gerald Parker.

Left, Mrs Mack (Gwyneth Guthrie) instructing Mr McPherson (John Young) in Scottish dancing.

Below, Archie is obviously in trouble with the arm of the law as well as his own! Director Jim McCann lines up a scene between Constable McPhee (Stewart Bishop), Archie Menzies (Paul Kermack) and Sergeant Murray (James MacDonald).

Jean McTaggart, for some years the house-keeper at Inverdarroch is a widow whose deafness afflicts her only when she doesn't want to hear. She reads teacups with remarkable accuracy, though frequently mis-interpreting what she sees.

Jean Faulds, who plays Mrs McTaggart, has worked in the theatre in Scotland and on film, radio and television over more years than she cares to remember. She has three daughters and numerous grandchildren.

Leslie Maxwell, a reporter on a big Glasgow-based newspaper spent a lot of time in the early days in Glendarroch trying to discover the plans of the German developers who had just taken over the estate.

He was played by Andrew Robertson.

Klaus Meier, the second German industrialist to own Glendarroch estate eventually went bankrupt and, benign character though he was, his influence was removed from Glendarroch.

Frederick Bartman played Klaus Meier.

Archie Menzies worked at the Big House man and boy for as long as anyone can remember. An expert at avoiding work he spent most of his time drinking tea in the office. Archie's ambition in life was to make a fast and easy buck and his attempts to achieve this ranged from opening a book on any event it is possible to make a bet on, to trying to persuade innocent people to part with money for a botched up job. One of his most financially productive, if fleeting, ploys concerned his discovery of the illicit still worked by Old Angus many years before. Several large butts of beautiful whisky were hidden in an underground cavern, and Archie began to sell it by the bottleful to the local crofters and farmers. The police got to hear about it. Forewarned, Archie and the locals tried to empty the barrels into as many empty bottles as they could find before the police arrived. But the barrels overturned and rolled down the hill, discharging their precious load and smashing to matchwood at the bottom.

Paul Kermack was educated at the Wade Academy in Anstruther and the Rose Bruford drama school in London. Destined for a singing career he realised early that his voice wasn't quite good enough to get to the very top of the operatic tree and, rather than settle for second best, he turned to full-time acting instead. In a long career, spanning most theatres in Scotland, he spent fifteen years in Scottish Television soap operas, starting with Jock Nesbit in *Garnock Way* and following that with Archie Menzies in *Take the High Road* until his sudden and tragic death in March 1990 robbed the series of one of its longest-serving and best-loved characters.

Claire Millar/Kerr came to Glendarroch as the district nurse some time after Jean Semple left. When she first arrived she made all her visits on a bicycle – which Inverdarroch ran over almost on her first day. She accused him of clumsiness and he bought her a new bicycle in recompense. This softened her attitude towards him. When he was injured under a tractor and broke his leg it was during his convalescence that she and Inverdarroch became very close. Inverdarroch discovered the reason for her not using the car which was provided. She had been driving a car involved in an accident in which her parents were killed. Inverdarroch helped her to banish her fear of driving, they became engaged and eventually married. But the marriage was not a success and later, when Sneddon too was injured Claire, dissatisfied with the way things were going at home, began a passionate affair

Right, the expert lead-swinger Archie Menzies (Paul Kermack) looks as if he is hatching yet another scheme for making a little easy money.

Below, Julie Miller queries a production point as cameraman Malcolm Campbell lines up a shot. In the story Nurse Millar has just arrived to attend to Inverdarroch (John Stahl) who has been injured in an accident with his tractor.

with him which everyone in the neighbourhood became aware of except Inverdarroch. In the end, lacking the courage to choose between Sneddon and Inverdarroch Claire simply left the district, never to return.

Claire Millar was played by Julie Miller who comes from Edinburgh and trained at the Queen Margaret College there. She has toured Scotland with Jimmy Logan, appeared at the Byre Theatre in St Andrews and has extensive experience in the theatre, having played roles ranging from Laura in *The Glass Menagerie* to principal boy in pantomime.

Obadiah Arthur Murdoch, clerk to the Kirk Session and general poacher is a well-known Glendarroch character who has spent most of his time being put in his place by Mrs Mack. He is a breeder of dogs for shepherds and has a thriving export business. For a long time no one knew what the 'O' in Mr Murdoch's signature, 'O. A. Murdoch', stood for, as he simply used 'Arthur' as his Christian name. Since the embarrassed Murdoch refused categorically to tell anyone, Archie Menzies found out from the Kirk records and opened a book on the subject. The winner of the competition to guess the name was Donald Lachlan who correctly chose Obadiah. Mr Murdoch's poaching has on many occasions got him into trouble. Once, when Eddie Ramsay, on the run from the army, was living rough in the woods, Murdoch shot him by mistake and nearly faced a charge. Mr Murdoch fell madly in love with Mrs Mack's sister, Florence, and even got to the point of asking her to marry him. But she, deliberately misunderstanding, thought he was declaring his love for her sister, Mary. This made Mr Murdoch retreat in haste and disarray.

Robert Trotter, who plays Mr Murdoch, made his first stage appearance as a wolf cub in the Gang Show at Dumbarton Burgh Hall in 1939.

Thereafter he won many prizes as a boy soprano. That seemed to be the peak, because after service in the Royal Navy he returned to teach English at Bellahouston Academy and then Drama at Glasgow University. But from there it was a simple step into full-time acting which began in radio drama – he was with the BBC Rep in 1978 – and then into theatre, where he has had an exciting career opening up new venues and producing unusual plays all over Scotland. After that he moved into television. He says the highlight of *Take the High Road* so far for him was the episode where he fell off the ladder in the village hall and ended up being discovered by the minister on the floor with Mrs Mack.

Sergeant Murray is the long-suffering head of the local police force. He is based in Auchtarne, but his patch covers Glendarroch where he is frequently in evidence.

James MacDonald and his wife Rebecca live in Prestwick and they have two children, Cameron and Joanne. Jimmy has a B.A. from the Open University and most members of the company remember the days when he sat in the green room between rehearsing scenes with his books open on the table in front of him, studying for his degree. As an ex-policeman himself he brings to the role of Sergeant Murray a very strong element of authenticity, and when the sergeant is not in evidence in the programme, Jimmy is either touring with a variety show, *Breath of Scotland*, which he has done for the last two years, or, during the past eight years appearing in pantomime at Christmas. He has appeared in many Scottish Television and BBC productions from Scotland and in between all this activity he especially enjoys swimming and holidaying in Spain – his favourite place – or entertaining and breadmaking. He formed the Gaberlunzie folk group and records on the Pye label.

Left, Eddie Ramsay (Robin Cameron), the father of Sheila Lamont's (Lesley Fitz-Simons) forthcoming baby, obviously wonders if she is wearing enough padding!

Right, a proud James MacDonald wearing his Sergeant Murray uniform with a mortar board instead of his cap on the occasion of his gaining a degree from the Open University.

Jackie Ogilvie's father owned an estate in the north east of Scotland where Douglas Dunbar had been factor before taking the job of factor at Glendarroch. Jackie followed him there and persuaded him to come back to her father's estate, which he did, and they got married.

Jackie Ogilvie was played by Hazel McBride.

Rev. Gerald Parker is the autocratic minister of St Ninian's in Auchtarne who took over Glendarroch Church when Mr McPherson announced his retirement. Mr Parker is deeply resented by the people of Glendarroch, so much so that most of the Kirk elders resigned on his taking the charge, and it was left to Michael Ross to re-recruit them later. There is little charity or Christian humility in Mr Parker's sermons and when he insisted on the endangered witch's tree on church land being cut down, everyone expected some kind of disaster. It was Mr Parker himself whom disaster struck when the trailer carrying the cut down tree passed over his foot, breaking several bones. There were those who said that justice had been done.

Paul Young, who plays Mr Parker, was born in Edinburgh and made his professional stage debut as Tiny Tim in a production of *A Christmas Carol* at the Gateway Theatre in 1953. Shortly after that he played the young Geordie in *Geordie* and from there his career has never looked back. Film work includes *Chato's Land* with Jack Palance and Charles Bronson and *Madame Sin* with Bette Davis and Robert Wagner. Most recently seen with Penelope Keith in *No Job for a Lady*, Paul is a keen angler and has represented Scotland in the National Trout Fly Fishing Team for several years. He is married to Radio Clyde broadcaster Sheila Duffy and they live in Glasgow with their two daughters, Hannah and Kate.

Roger Primrose, a failed businessman, was a guest at the Ardnacraig Hotel. By faking an accident caused, he claimed, by Fiona Cunningham's negligence, he managed to get free board and lodging for a long time before Sorry Watson found out what he was up to. Sorry persuaded him that however unfair the business world had been to him it did not justify his trying to ruin Fiona's business too. Mr Primrose left the hotel, paying his bill in full before he went.

He was played by Norman Bird.

Eddie Ramsay, the son of Fraser Ramsay, the local ne'er-do-well, was tarred with the same brush as his father. He made Sheila Lamont pregnant after saving her from the unwelcome attentions of her ex-boyfriend, Frank Riddle, he broke into the till in Blair's Store and he stole the money from the organising tent at the local Highland Games. But when this was discovered, Brian Blair and Sorry Watson, both seeing some latent good in Eddie, gave him the chance to redeem himself. Sorry offered to pay for what he had stolen, take Eddie back to Shetland with him, and find him a job to enable him to repay the debt. Eddie agreed. Later he returned, a reformed character, only to be disappointed again when Sheila had their baby adopted without telling him. Yet he felt conscience-stricken at depriving Sheila of the prospects of further education and a chance in life. He entered the Glendarroch Hill Race that was being revived to raise money for a lifeboat on the loch, but failed to win the prize he wanted to give to her. Sheila was touched by this and their friendship developed under the eye of Jock Campbell whose cottage Eddie was now living in. When Jock, who was going blind, decided to move into an old folks' home in Auchtarne, he did so on condition that Eddie got the cottage and married Sheila. They married and lived for a time in the cottage, but Sheila, still intent on completing her education, began to study for an Open University degree. This entailed going away to a week's Summer School where she had an affair with one of the lecturers. Eddie discovered this and, as at the same time he was being accused of stealing Mrs Mack's purse from the village hall – it was eventually found behind the boiler where she had dropped it – he left Glendarroch to join the army. Later he returned, having gone absent without leave after knocking down a vicious sergeant who had been bullying recruits and he now faced a court martial. His CO, however, came to Glendarroch to persuade him to return, since the truth about the sergeant had come out, the sergeant himself was awaiting a court martial and Eddie was required to give evidence.

Eddie Ramsay is played by Robin Cameron who, since gaining an M.A. at Glasgow University has worked in theatres all round Scotland and appeared in many television plays and schools programmes.

Fraser Ramsay was Eddie Ramsay's dissolute father, a drunk and a wastrel who had never cared for his son at all, leaving Eddie bitter and rejected.

Fraser Ramsay was played by the well-known Scottish comedian, Hector Nicol, until his death in 1985.

Joe Reilly, the layabout husband of Moira Reilly came to Glendarroch to avoid being beaten up by a back-street moneylender with whom he had become entangled. His financial problems were due to his fatal attraction to backing horses. He could never understand why his brother-in-law, Inverdarroch, had no interest in this pursuit and regarded him as a clodhopping stick-in-the-mud.

Ian Bleasdale played Joe Reilly.

Moira Reilly was Moira Kerr, Inverdarroch's sister. She married Joe and Inverdarroch believed they were living a comfortable and settled life in Lancashire. When Moira took Inverdarroch's bank book containing his life savings he discovered the truth. To pay off Reilly's threatening moneylender, Inverdarroch drew the money himself, gave it to Moria and told her and Joe to go away and never come back.

Anne Kidd played Moira Reilly.

Mark Ritchie bought *The Auchtarne Herald* from its previous owner after his wife died and he no longer wanted to work on a Glasgow newspaper. He raised the standard of the paper considerably. He was principally instrumental in uncovering a great deal of the dirt on Councillor Robert Watt, Glendarroch's regional councillor who, during many years of unopposed election to the council had come to regard the position as his right while he pursued his shady wheeling and dealing. Watt paid Andy Semple to beat up Ritchie in his office, and Semple was only prevented from doing Ritchie serious injury by the untimely arrival in the office of Sheila Ramsay. From then until the election Ritchie worked tirelessly to discredit Watt and it was mainly due to him that Watt was arrested immediately after the announcement that he had beaten Isabel Blair by a handful of votes. Watt, however, got his revenge by threatening to found a free sheet newspaper in Glendarroch that would almost certainly put *The Auchtarne Herald* out of business.

Mark Ritchie was played by Peter Raffan who comes from the north east of Scotland and trained at the Royal Scottish Academy of Music and Drama. He has extensive experience of television, having played Ewan Tavendale in BBC Scotland's production of *Grey Granite* by Lewis Grassic Gibbon, and has worked in the theatre everywhere between Inverness and the Borders.

Hugh Robbie, the local drystane dyker, took on Eric Ross-Gifford as a partner to help him when he had broken his wrist and couldn't work himself.

Joe Greig played Hugh Robbie.

Michael Ross was Rev. Gerald Parker's assistant when he first came to Glendarroch and quickly became integrated into the local community. After some time working under Mr Parker he decided the ministry was not for him and went back to his former love, farming, becoming manager of the Glendarroch Home Farm.

Michael Ross is played by Gordon MacArthur who comes from Lanarkshire and trained at the Guildhall School of Music and Drama. He has worked extensively in theatre and television and is a scratch golfer.

Eric Ross-Gifford is the only child of Sir John and Lady Margaret Ross-Gifford. Born in London and raised in the high-flying social setting Lady Margaret favoured, he was expensively educated and took a fairly ordinary degree at Oxford. Eric married Joanna Simpson, much against Lady Margaret's wishes, since her parents were 'in trade', though Sir John appreciated Joanna's common sense and believed she would be good for Eric. Sir John left the estate to the two of them to run for him. This was not a particularly good idea, since neither had the knowledge or the experience to undertake the job. Eric made several basic mistakes, the principal one being to appoint Sneddon factor of Glendarroch. After Lady Margaret left him, Sir John was going to sell the estate again, but Eric and Joanna asked him for a year to try to put it on to a paying footing. Reluctantly he

agreed. They failed to meet their target and Sir John asked Fiona Cunningham to return and act as factor. This she did, while Eric and Joanna took over the Ardnacraig Hotel.

Richard Greenwood, who plays Eric, was born in South Wales and educated at Trinity College, Glenalmond and St Andrews University before turning to the acting profession. He has appeared at the Wolsey Theatre in Ipswich and the Pitlochry Festival Theatre, and in many television plays including *The Campbells* for Scottish Television and *The Houseman's Tale* for the BBC before landing the job of playing the wimpish son of the Big House. He lists his hobbies as fishing, board games, learning to play golf and doing crossword puzzles, at which he is becoming something of an addict in breaks in rehearsals. Single at the moment, Richard provided the first *Take the High Road* 'in-house' wedding when he married Gillian McNeill who plays Lynne McNeil in July this year.

Joanna Ross-Gifford was born Joanna Simpson. Her parents are Scottish and she was educated in Scotland and at Oxford where she met Eric Ross-Gifford. Marriage to Eric was not easy and there were times when Joanna almost despaired of ever getting him to work seriously and productively. During one of their periodic rows she spent the night at a distant hotel with Ruari Galbraith and later found herself to be pregnant. Eric was delighted, and Joanna was faced with the dilemma of not knowing whether to tell him there was just the slightest possibility that the child might not be his. Discretion was the better part of valour and she kept silent. But her guilt preyed on her mind to such an extent that, thanks to a series of unhappy accidents, she miscarried. Eric was devastated and it was only then that she finally confessed. Eric was furious and returned to his mother in London.

The new family outside Glendarroch House: Joanna Simpson (Tamara Kennedy), Sir John Ross-Gifford (Michael Browning), his wife, Lady Margaret (Jan Waters) and their son, Eric (Richard Greenwood).

Eventually he came back and they both made their peace. The truth was that while Joanna could manage life without Eric, Eric found it very difficult to manage life without Joanna.

Tamara Kennedy plays Joanna Ross-Gifford. Before coming to the programme she had already made a name for herself in a host of television and radio plays and has worked in many Scottish theatres from the smallest – the Mull Little Theatre – to among the largest – the Lyceum in Edinburgh – playing a wide variety of parts from Fairy Bowbells in *Dick Whittington* at Perth to Kate in *The Taming of the Shrew* and Titania in *A Midsummer Night's Dream* in open-air midnight performances in Kelvingrove Park in Glasgow. She was educated at St Denis School in Edinburgh and graduated M.A. in English and Drama at Glasgow University. Tamara married Robin Barbour, a social worker, last year. She is a splendid artist – she designed the *Take the High Road* Christmas Card two years ago – and is painstakingly revising the pictures and text of a children's book which has been occupying her for four years. In the midst of all this activity she still finds time for reading, swimming and drinking cappuccino in coffee shops whenever possible. She is not the only famous member of her family – her great great grandfather was Sir William Henry Perkin, the chemist who discovered the dye purple.

Sir John Ross-Gifford bought Glendarroch from Fiona Cunningham when inheritance tax forced her to put it up for sale. Sir John, an expatriate Scot had made his fortune in the business world in London. He bought the estate hoping it might help to restore his failing marriage and also give his somewhat useless son Eric the purpose in life he seemed unable to achieve in the social whirl of London. But it didn't work. Lady Margaret hated it, Eric proved himself again and again to be incompetent, in spite of Joanna's support. Sir John eventually decided to gift the estate to Eric and Joanna so that they would not have to face death duties, while he returned to his business world in London.

Apart from *Take the High Road*, Michael Browning who played Sir John Ross-Gifford, has appeared in many other soap operas, including *Emmerdale*, *Coronation Street* and *Crossroads*. He has worked extensively in theatres throughout England. He lives in London.

Lady Margaret Ross-Gifford was not really the right partner for Sir John. He had the money, she had the aristocratic connections, but they didn't blend. She detested her removal from the London scene to this remote and uncivilised part of the Highlands.

Jan Waters, who played Lady Margaret, was born in Bournemouth and trained as a classical singer before combining straight and musical theatre in the 1960s. She has worked in the West End in such shows as *Do Re Mi* at the Prince of Wales, *High Spirits* at the Savoy, *The Young Visiters* at the Piccadilly and *Showboat* at the Adelphi. She appeared in Michael Frayn's two-handed award-winning play *Benefactors* with John Alderton at the Vaudeville and has toured for the British Council in the Middle East, playing Eliza Doolittle in *Pygmalion* and Portia in *The Merchant of Venice*. Jan lives in London with actor Philip York and their two children Lucy and Ben.

Lady William Ross-Gifford, Sir John's mother, is a formidable lady who owns an estate in the far north of Scotland from which she used to make frequent forays to Glendarroch to create alarm and mayhem. She insisted on calling Sir John Bobo in front of all and sundry to his intense embarrassment.

Lady William was played by the doyenne of the Scottish theatre and television industry, Madeleine Christie. After a long theatrical career in Scotland, Madeleine now lives in London with her daughter and son-in-law and their family and she is a great-grandmother. The house, she says, is very full but never dull. Her son was Controller of BBC Scotland for many years. Coming into *Take the High Road*, says Madeleine, enabled her to fulfil the second of her two remaining ambitions: to appear in a soap opera. Her first was to do pub theatre, and this she achieved a month or two before coming back to Scotland to play Lady William.

Mrs Russell was the first housekeeper at Letir-Falloch, but she left when she couldn't take Sneddon's rudeness any longer.

Mrs Russell was played by Fay Lenore.

Sam Scanlon is a sharp but honest wheeler and dealer, a man who can turn his hand to anything in the building line and who has made a fortune doing so. He met Irene Lamont in Glasgow and she, in some embarrassment at his rough exterior, brought him to Glendarroch to introduce him to her daughter, Sheila. At that time the Kirk Session was seriously worried about the condition of the bell tower in the church, and the estimates they had had for essential and substantial repairs were far higher than they could afford. Sam examined the tower and decided that if they had enough money to buy the materials and if they provided the labour, he would direct the repairs and at least put the tower into a reasonable condition for the next few years. This endeared him to the locals and the job was done. Eventually Sam persuaded Irene to marry him. The wedding took place in Glasgow during the Garden Festival and was the highlight of the Glendarroch year.

Stewart Preston plays Sam Scanlon.

Andy Semple was the manager of the Glendarroch sawmill but lost his job for cooking the books and absconding with a lot of cash. Thereafter he turned more and more to crime, so much so that his wife took the children away and never returned. He has been in and out of jail all his life.

The trouble with a part like Andy Semple is that as a really bad lot, he spends much of his time in jail, so *Take the High Road* doesn't see enough of Alexander Morton, who plays him. But then Sandy works so much in the theatre and in other television shows that he is not often available. He has worked with almost every theatre company in Scotland, large and small, and he has also a host of television credits to his name.

Jean Semple, the wife of Andy Semple, was also for a time the district nurse. They had two children and Jean took them with her when she left Andy Semple and Glendarroch for a new life in the south.

Jeni Giffen played Jean Semple.

Lorna Seton had an unhappy marriage and, although there was a daughter, she left her and her husband to go home to Glendarroch where she was born. For many years she was the competent and efficient secretary of Glendarroch estate, first under Elizabeth Cunningham, then under Fiona and finally under the Ross-Giffords. To begin with she lived with her demanding and utterly selfish mother. To provide the little luxuries she believed her mother needed, Lorna lifted money from the petty cash in the office. She was discovered by Ken Calder who confronted her mother. Thanks to her, he told her, Lorna was getting into debt. If she went to jail, who would look after her then? he asked. Lorna's mother agreed to change her ways. She died shortly afterwards and Lorna moved into a cottage in the village, discovering later that Ken had been after the same cottage. She and Ken agreed to share it. He lived there for some time and affection grew between them. They thought of regularising the situation and getting married, but decided against it, and some time later Ken returned to the bottle and Lorna felt that she had been saved at the last moment.

Joan Alcorn plays Lorna Seton.

Harry Shaw is the real name of the great pop star Vincent. About to embark on a major American tour, he did not want his wife, Sally, with him, so he sent her in the care of Davie Sneddon to Letir-Falloch which he had just bought. Later, Harry bought a half share in the Ardnacraig Hotel and helped Fiona to run it. Sally who was suing Harry for divorce had a private enquiry agent planted in the hotel. The man believed he had found enough evidence for her to cite Fiona as co-respondent and claim half his entire estate. Harry, on the other hand, issued a counterclaim for divorce on the grounds of Sally's misconduct with Jimmy Blair while he was in America. The principal witness to this was Sneddon, who claimed as his price security of tenure as factor of Letir-Falloch and an increase in wages.

Laurie McNicol plays Harry Shaw.

Sally Shaw was sent to Letir-Falloch by her husband, Harry, in the care of Davie Sneddon. She became involved in a passionate affair with Jimmy Blair, an affair his parents totally disapproved of. She abandoned Jimmy to return to her husband in America following his injury in a car crash.

Judith Sweeney plays Sally Shaw.

Davie Sneddon is the villain of the piece. An Irishman, brought to Letir-Falloch as factor-

manager by Harry Shaw, Sneddon has always had bad relations with the people of Glendarroch. When Eric Ross-Gifford offered him the job of factor at Glendarroch, Sneddon retaliated by getting rid of the estate workers who had been mainly responsible for his loss of face at Letir-Falloch. Top of his list was Bob Taylor, the water bailiff, who eventually left Glendarroch altogether, to take up a new job as manager of a fish farm in the north of Scotland. But Sneddon overstepped the mark when he found Lady Margaret in a compromising situation with Harry Somers, an old flame from London. He threatened to tell Sir John if she didn't support his demand for security of tenure after Eric had left the running of the estate to Sir John himself. As Lady Margaret was intending to leave Sir John this threat held no terrors for her. She told Sir John and he, also finding that Sneddon had illegally maintained his job at Letir-Falloch, sacked him immediately. The people of Glendarroch were freed from Sneddon's machinations and he returned to Letir-Falloch. His affair with Claire Kerr, Inverdarroch's wife, caused Inverdarroch to come seeking him with a shotgun.

Derek Lord, who plays Davie Sneddon, emigrated to Australia at the age of twenty and for six months hitchhiked around the continent, cutting sugarcane and lumping wheat before he joined a touring company in Western Australia. Later he toured South Australia, then moved to Melbourne. He returned to Belfast to work at the Lyric Theatre before moving to London. He has worked at the Abbey Theatre in Dublin and at the Royal Court and the Mermaid Theatre in London. He married Irish actress Lana McDonnell and they have a son, Barry. After his marriage he settled in Dublin. He played Burke in a play about Burke and Hare at the Tron Theatre in Glasgow, was seen in it by one of the *Take the High Road* writers, and was asked to play Davie Sneddon.

Drew Sneddon is Davie Sneddon's son whose mind was poisoned against his father by his mother. He came to Glendarroch to seek out his father and proved himself to be an even more obnoxious character. While there he got into trouble with Jean Kennedy and with the police. Eventually, feigning death in the loch, he was discovered in hiding and kicked out by the police and also by his father.

He was played by Peter Richey.

Kathleen Sneddon was sent by her father to stay with her uncle Davie Sneddon because she was keeping company with a boy her parents didn't approve of. What Sneddon didn't know was that she was pregnant and, out for a walk one day she went into premature labour. She was found in this state by Bob Taylor who carried her to the Lachlan croft, where Robert Forsyth, the vet, delivered her of twins, one of whom was dead. Sneddon, appalled by this, intended to sue Forsyth for malpractice, but Dr Wallace told Sneddon that a post mortem had revealed that the second baby had been dead before birth. Kathleen returned to her parents who had agreed that she should marry Tony, her boy friend. She asked Robert Forsyth if she might call her surviving daughter Kirsty after his wife and daughter.

Kathleen Sneddon was played by Hilary Reynolds.

Harry Somers was one of Lady Margaret's smart London friends, a presumed expert at hunting, shooting and fishing. He boasted he would catch old Greedy-guts, the giant pike that was ruining the fishing in the loch. Eric caught Greedy-guts instead and Harry lost a good deal of face. Lady Margaret was extremely attracted to him, and he to her, though his interest in her sprang more from a desire to anger Sir John.

Derek Waring played Harry Somers.

Jane Steedman was a surveyor who worked firstly for a firm in Edinburgh before transferring to the employment of Max Langemann to do a survey of Glendarroch House, advise on the costs of turning it into a luxury hotel and the whole estate into a holiday complex.

She was played by Ingrid Haffner.

Stephen was the lecturer whom Sheila Ramsay met at her Open University summer school. She had an affair with him, although he was married. Later Stephen reappeared in Glendarroch, saying that he had left his wife and wanted to marry Sheila. She refused.

He was played by James Telfer.

Jamie Stewart, Morag Stewart's father, ran the croft that marched with Dougal Lachlan's, but left most of the work on it to Morag. Jamie eventually contracted Altzheimer's disease and for a long time Morag nursed him without telling anyone. In the end he was put in a home in Auchtarne and is still there.

Jamie Stewart was played by James Copeland, who has spent fifty years in the theatre, films and television. Perhaps his best remembered role was the mate in *The Maggie*. He has given a succession of brilliant performances over the years, one of the most memorable being that of Jamie Stewart in his latter days.

Morag Stewart, the daughter of Jamie Stewart, is the butt of much of the neighbouring crofters' crude humour. But Morag is no fool and runs her croft possibly with greater efficiency than the men, though none of them would admit it, least of all Dougal Lachlan.

A shepherd's life is a solitary one and Morag Stewart (Jeannie Fisher), alone since her father's departure to a home, gains comfort from herding her sheep on the hill above Glendarroch.

For a long time people tried to pair Morag off with Dougal, but neither of them cared for the other sufficiently to marry although it would have been a highly convenient arrangement. Morag in fact has a very soft spot for Inverdarroch whose happiness means more to her than anything else, and she was mainly instrumental in persuading Claire to marry him because that was what would make him happy. She even agreed to be Claire's bridesmaid.

Morag is played by Jeannie Fisher, who was born in Glasgow and trained at the Royal Scottish Academy of Music and Drama. She has worked in the theatre throughout the country and in radio and television. She commutes between flats in London and Edinburgh which she shares with her cat, Floozie.

Willie Stewart, a cousin of Jamie Stewart's was scheming to make Jamie leave him the Stewart croft instead of Morag.

He was played by Walter Carr.

Lady Strathmorris, the wife of Lord Strathmorris, is a slightly empty-headed woman and a friend of Elizabeth Cunningham's. She is well aware of the machinations of her husband but can do nothing about them.

She is played by Ellen McIntosh.

Lord Strathmorris, a neighbouring landowner, has on several occasions tried to swing dirty deals on Glendarroch. He was a member of the board set up by Langemann International to run the estate after the death of Sir Logan Peddie, and during its existence he attempted to push through many projects which would have benefited him personally. He was a thorn in the flesh of Elizabeth Cunningham for many years and later of Fiona.

Lord Strathmorris is played by Bernard Gallagher.

Miss Symonds is the local primary school teacher. At one time there was a rumour that she had been transferred from a neighbouring school because she had assaulted a pupil there. The truth was that the pupil in question had actually been threatening another pupil with a lino gouge. When Miss Symonds had managed to pull him away, he had fallen and damaged a kidney. The enquiry had exonerated her and in fact praised her for her action. After all this came out she thought of resigning from the Glendarroch Primary School, but her pupils persuaded her to stay.

She is played by Harriet Buchan.

Bob Taylor was one of the three sons of a water bailiff on an estate on the other side of Auchtarne. He was the Glendarroch water bailiff and responsible for stocking the lochs and rivers on the estate and organising fishing parties. He married Alice McEwan, Dougal Lachlan's sister-in-law, and after her miscarriage they looked after Donald Lachlan for many years until Dougal remarried.

He was played by Iain Agnew.

Lily Taylor is the widow of Bob Taylor's brother, Matthew, who had gone south early in his life and married an English wife. A highly romantic person, Lily believes the best of everybody and thinks living in Glendarroch is the closest thing to paradise. After her first visit she wrote a book about the area called *This Is My Glen* which became a best-seller, was serialised in a woman's magazine, and brought her a lot of money. She became attracted to Inverdarroch during her visits and when Inverdarroch was in danger of being put out of his farm she bought it for him, an action which effectively ended any chance of a romance between them. Lily eventually married her agent.

She is played by Thelma Rogers.

Dr Alexander Wallace's father was the local doctor and Sandy became his partner after graduating in medicine. An old-fashioned country general practitioner he is, as most such doctors are, adept at the practical business of helping people in distress or discomfort without the usual easy direct referral to hospital.

Michael Elder, who plays Dr Wallace comes from a medical background. His father was a general practitioner as is his sister. The reason he became an actor and a writer is that he faints at the sight of blood. He has been married for more than thirty-five years to Scottish actress Sheila Donald, and they have two sons, neither in the slightest degree interested in the acting business, and four grandchildren at the last count, though that number will shortly be added to. He has been a writer for the programme since the first series and is also one of the script editors. He has also written this book, and has great difficulty in keeping all these hats on his head at the same time.

Sorry Watson is a local man who was left a croft by an uncle in Shetland. Sorry took over the croft and sold it for a phenomenal sum to an oil company who needed the land. Sorry discovered a hidden ability in dealing with complex financial matters and over the years built up a huge fortune, though it never changed the mild, shy manner which gave him his nickname. He has done much for Glendarroch over the years, though he no longer lives there.

Sorry Watson is played by Ron Paterson.

Councillor Robert Watt represents Glendarroch on the regional council. He is a crooked politician, a wheeler and dealer and did nothing to justify his unopposed election. When Isabel Blair stood against him at the local elections he employed many dubious means to prevent her campaign from getting off the ground, but Isabel failed to beat him by only a handful of votes. Watt was arrested for not declaring his interests in some firms which were negotiating for council contracts, and although the case against him was eventually dropped for lack of evidence, his security of tenure was severely dented.

Councillor Watt is played by David McKail.

Malky Wilson was in prison with Brian Blair. He came to Glendarroch to get sanctuary from some tough customers who were looking for him after his release from prison because he had double-crossed them before going in. Brian and Isabel did not dare to expose him to the police for fear that he would declare that the Blairs were harbouring a known criminal and that would have meant Brian's immediate return to prison. Eventually it was Ken Calder who discovered that Malky was an alcoholic. Ken managed to get him helpless on drink and took him to the psychiatric hospital in Glasgow where he himself had been dried out.

Malky Wilson is played by Freddie Boardley.

Oggie Wilson left Glendarroch at an early age to work on the Outer Isles ferries, but returned when there seemed a chance of picking up Morag Stewart and her croft. S plausible character with a silver tongue he went off with Hamish McNeil's niece Heather when his hopes of Morag came to naught.

He was played by Sean Scanlon.

Mrs Woods fell on hard times when her husband died young and left her with little to live on. She takes in bed and breakfast guests during the tourist season and is prominent in local affairs.

Mrs Woods is played by Primrose Milligan.

Colin Young was one half of a confidence trickster partnership, though his wife Hazel was the brains.

He was played by George Howell.

Hazel Young, Colin Young's wife, passed herself off as his sister and gained access to Letir-Falloch by applying for the job of house-keeper. She made Sneddon fall for her and at the same time Dougal Lachlan. Eventually she and Colin cleaned Letir-Falloch out and left with the booty. They were almost the only two people to succeed in deceiving Davie Sneddon completely.

Hazel Young was played by Una MacNab.

Nikki Zaharoff was a Russian double agent sent by MI6 to Sir John for vetting. Sir John had known him during his days in the diplomatic service. He was eventually returned to his own people.

Michael Sheard played Nikki Zaharoff.

THE FUTURE

By the beginning of November 1990, when the fourteenth series of *Take the High Road* finishes in the studio, 831 episodes will have been recorded.

People who have followed the programme through its first ten years and into its eleventh will have been aware of major changes. Some have viewed the new series with dismay, some with anger, but most have enjoyed the changes, accepted the new format and continued watching.

Many of these changes took place in response to changes which are occurring in the area around the village of Luss. A new golf course is being built at Loch Lomond, a major international course designed by Tom Weiskopf and, as it has always been *Take the High Road*'s policy to use whatever facilities might be available for filming, the golf course was a natural.

Ten years is a long time and it was perhaps not practical to believe that the old cosy *Take the High Road* of 1980 could continue unaltered into the 1990s. That way stagnation lies.

Television in this country is facing a major and controversial upheaval through the Government's demands for changes in the method of providing programmes for the public. No one knows at present what these changes will entail, so Scottish Television's longest-running drama contribution to the national network awaits, as does everyone else, the resolution of the future.

IN MEMORIAM

Victor Carin, Script Editor   1981

Clarke Tait, Producer   1984

Hector Nicol, *Fraser Ramsay*   1985

Pat Daly, *Father Joseph Houston*   1987

Bill Henderson, *Ken Calder*   1988

Jeremy Hare, Unit Manager   1989

Paul Kermack, *Archie Menzies*   1990